DEATH

&

DYING

EDITED
by

COLM KEANE

Published in association with
Radio Telefís Éireann

MERCIER PRESS

MERCIER PRESS
5 French Church Street, Cork
16 Hume Street, Dublin 1

© The contributors, 1995

A CIP is available for this book from the British Library

ISBN 1 85635 113 0

10 9 8 7 6 5 4 3 2 1

Printed in Ireland by Colour Books Ltd.

CONTENTS

LIST OF CONTRIBUTORS

Colm Keane   Senior Producer, Radio Telefís
Éireann.

Anthony Clare   Medical Director, St Patrick's
Hospital, Dublin; Clinical Professor
of Psychiatry, Trinity College,
Dublin.

Aideen O'Keeffe   Senior Social Worker, St John of God
Hospital, Stillorgan, Co. Dublin, and
Private Practice.

Phil Larkin   Community Home Care Nurse,
Galway Hospice Foundation,
Galway.

Fin Breatnach   Consultant Paediatric Oncologist,
Our Lady's Hospital for Sick
Children, Dublin.

Margo Wrigley   Consultant Psychiatrist in the
Psychiatry of Old Age, James
Connolly Memorial Hospital,
Dublin.

Anthony O'Flaherty   Consultant Psychiatrist, St Patrick's
Hospital, Dublin.

Michael J. Kelleher   Consultant Psychiatrist and Clinical
Director, St Anne's Hospital, Cork.

Kevin Connolly   Consultant Paediatrician,
Portiuncula Hospital, Ballinasloe,
Co. Galway.

John Donohoe   Clinical Psychologist, specialising in Grief and Bereavement, Private Practice, Ballinasloe, Co. Galway.

Nuala Harmey   Senior Medical Social Worker, The Children's Hospital, Temple Street, Dublin.

Brendan Doody   Registrar in Child and Adolescent Psychiatry, Eastern Health Board, Dublin.

Tony O'Brien   Medical Director, Marymount Hospice, Cork.

INTRODUCTION

COLM KEANE

NUMBNESS, DISBELIEF, GUILT, ANGER, denial, pain, loneliness, fear, self-blame and the ambivalent feelings of love and hate are just some of the emotions that can result from bereavement.

They can be accompanied by resentment, frustration, anxiety, sadness, confusion, remorse and the feeling of regret that words were left unsaid or unspoken.

Family life may be disrupted. Life patterns and relationships are changed. Future plans may be interrupted and aspirations left in disarray.

All of these, while common and normal, can cause intense and frightening reactions in the bereaved. They can give rise to serious distress, leaving the person heartbroken and in physical or psychological pain.

As Professor Anthony Clare says, 'None of this betokens mental instability. It is our very essence coming to terms with loss. Yet it is important to recognise that no one who has lost someone very close and very dear to them is ever the same again.'

IN ONE WAY OR another, we are all affected by death. We all must cope with bereavement at some stage in our lives. And the likelihood is that we will all experience grief.

This book is aimed at people who wish to understand the process involved. The bereavement may follow the death of a parent, brother, sister, child, friend or spouse.

The death may have been sudden, unanticipated, peaceful, violent, painful or tragic. The resulting grief may be delayed, prolonged or easily managed.

The hope is that through reading this book, we can come to understand that grief is not something abnormal or to be feared like an illness. Rather, it is a normal and inevitable step in our journey through life.

The chapter titles and content have been selected to help us comprehend the sometimes complex emotions and reactions which are commonly encountered.

Chapter headings have been chosen to match the programme titles of the RTE Radio 1 series *Death and Dying*.

It is hoped that the practical information provided in the following pages and the real-life stories related in the radio series will help demystify the uneasy and distressing sense of loss that follows the death of a loved one.

NO DEATH IS MORE tragic than the death of a child. Nor is there any experience more moving than listening to a parent describe how such a death has occurred. The pain and sadness that result from the loss of someone so young and so innocent can be unbearable and indescribable.

'The impact of death in childhood', says Dr Fin Breatnach, 'is out of all proportion to its incidence in terms of the number of people affected by the death and the appalling severity of the effects.'

This sense of tragedy and loss can be even more pronounced if the death follows a stillbirth – a form of death about which we can be dismissive and insensitive. Yet the impact of such a death causes a huge scar which can take a long time to heal, according to Dr Kevin Connolly.

'When death occurs in pregnancy, many of the usual responses – emptiness, low self-esteem and unbearable helplessness – result from a mother's feeling that she has lost a part of herself', Dr Connolly says.

THERE ARE MANY CONSEQUENCES which result from the death of a spouse, among them loss of income, loss of a partner to talk to and loss of status and friends. Other losses identified by Aideen O'Keeffe include the loss of a confidante to share troubles with and the loss of a companion for outings and social events.

The death of a loved partner is often described as one of the worst losses that we can experience. 'We spend time and effort building up a relationship with another person ... Then suddenly it ends – one partner dies and the other is bereft', Aideen O'Keeffe says.

Phil Larkin turns his attention to the death of a parent. He points out that for most people, a parent's death closes a chapter in their lives, one which draws them back to the emotional feelings of childhood.

'The death of someone as close to us as a parent can be a devastating blow to our feelings of security and safety', he says.

So what of death from old age? Dr Margo Wrigley informs us that most people now live until their mid- to late seventies. Furthermore, two-thirds of people who die do so in institutions.

'What this means is that death has become a relatively unfamiliar event since it is largely confined to old age, and those who die are unlikely to do so in their own homes ... the modern denial of death is in part related to the reduced opportunity to witness death and participate in its rituals', Dr Wrigley concludes.

DEATH MAY BE LIFE'S single certainty. Yet it strikes in unexpected and sometimes tragic ways. Take death by suicide or murder, for example. These topics are again tackled in the pages ahead.

The bewildering devastation, the stigmatisation, the spectacle, the gossip and anger that follow death by murder are examined by John Donohoe. Such a death challenges our concept of life as good, fair and just. 'It is not uncommon for people bereaved in this way to develop psychiatric problems, such as depression, anxiety and phobic reactions, alcoholism, suicidal behaviour and post-traumatic stress disorder', he concludes.

Suicide and homicide have something in common, argues Dr Michael Kelleher. A life is ended before its time, in circumstances that are often painful, rarely dignified and virtually always distressing if not patently harmful to the bereaved, he says.

'An initial or enduring response may be one of numbness

11

and indifference to many aspects of personal, professional and family life. What was important once may now be seen as trivial, and enthusiasm for life may be replaced by a sense of pointlessness and dread', he concludes.

Then there is the controversial issue of withdrawing treatment from a dying patient – an issue which can cause great emotional and intellectual distress.

Is there a difference between stopping treatment and never starting it or between withdrawing a treatment and actively assisting death?

'The resolution of these questions without doing violence to anyone's conscience is vital if we are to achieve a dignified death for our terminally-ill patients', Nuala Harmey says.

THE FOLLOWING CHAPTERS ALSO offer practical information and advice. There are two summary chapters at the end of the book which are devoted to this objective.

In 'Living with Dying', Dr Tony O'Brien gives advice on how families might respond to a diagnosis of progressive disease, such as cancer. 'Time becomes extremely precious. There is an opportunity for people to explore their relationships with themselves, with their families and friends and with their God,' he concludes.

In 'Coping with Death', Dr Brendan Doody takes us through the stages of grief. Mourning ends, he says, 'when the bereaved can truly accept that the person is gone and thoughts of the person do not produce pain ... We accept that the person is dead and not coming back. What is past is past and cannot be changed.'

Finally, the symptoms of abnormal grief are examined by Dr Anthony O'Flaherty. He describes the numbness and disbelief that lead to denial and prevent healing. Sometimes, he says, grief can be delayed for ten or more years.

'We cannot prevent bereavement', he argues, 'but an important preventive measure is to accept the inevitability of death and to prepare for it as we might prepare for any of life's other major traumas.'

I WOULD LIKE TO express my appreciation to the many people who helped in getting this project started. In particular, my thanks to Michael Littleton of RTE for his advice and encouragement. My thanks also to Professor Anthony Clare for his guidance and enthusiasm from the outset.

I would like to mention Tom Manning and Kevin Healy of RTE for their support. Also my gratitude to Mary Feehan and Maria O'Donovan of Mercier Press for their editing and publishing expertise.

My appreciation, as always, goes to Úna O'Hagan and Seán Keane for their continued persistence with my projects. Finally, to all the contributors and case-histories involved in the book and radio series, my sincere thanks.

COLM KEANE

DEATH AND DYING

PROFESSOR ANTHONY CLARE

ONE OF THE MORE attractive aspects of life in Ireland is how as a culture we accept and acknowledge death. Anyone caught as I have so often been in a Dublin traffic jam around 5:30 in the evening as a funeral cortège winds its way across rush-hour traffic will be struck at the importance still publicly granted to private grieving, the priority afforded to the rituals of death in the very midst of the hard, mercenary activities of earning a living, doing a day's work, keeping body and soul together. People are still moved to spare the time and show their respects to the dead, not merely dead family, relatives and close friends but work colleagues, schoolmates, even people they do not know personally but for whom they have admiration and respect.

Death in Ireland still commands curiosity, interest, explicit reference. Our culture has resisted trends elsewhere where death has increasingly been banished to hospital and institution, where the ritual of death has become ever more muted, where wakes are bland, hygienic and speedy affairs and where the bereaved are largely left to their own private thoughts – where death is at once private and hidden.

Death ignored might well be death denied. Nigel Llewellyn, a historian of death and dying, recently sardonically observed that the Victorians 'lingered over death but could not bring themselves to recognise the public existence of sexual relations; in the latter part of the twentieth century sex gradually became a subject for open discussion, but death seems more deeply buried than ever' (*The Art of Dying*, 1991).

SEX AND DEATH ARE seen in many cultures as rites of passage of equal importance. Psychology is conventionally associated in the public mind with an openness, even a preoccupation concerning sex whereas in truth the whole of modern psychology could be said to arise from thoughts about death. Surprisingly there are few books which handle the psychology of death directly. And yet the only certainty we share as human beings is that we all will die.

The real loss of innocence is not a child's discovery of sex but of death, of his or her own mortality, and the shattering realisation that almost invariably proceeds out of a dawning sense that the death of another, an animal, a relative, a friend, a parent is itself a portent of what, one day, will happen to oneself.

Death, which means many things, is most often articulated as an absence, a void, an emptiness. Experienced early enough, by a young child for example, the sudden, unexpected absence of a parent's death can be experienced as an abandonment. In turn, the absence and abandonment often lead to a sense of separation, of alienation which can mark that child for many years into adult life, can make every modest going-away a little death.

A RECENTLY BEREAVED INDIVIDUAL experiences symptoms closely resembling those of depressive disorders. Indeed Freud's own theory of the causes of depression, enunciated in a classic paper revealingly entitled 'Mourning and Melancholia', was based on such a similarity. There are three stages of normal mourning characteristically described.

The *first stage* is marked by a lack of emotional reaction or numbness. A feeling of unreality occurs which lasts from a few hours to a few days. Psychologists and psychiatrists are somewhat preoccupied with so-called abnormal grief reactions, pathological grieving, patterns of responding to death which become so protracted or extreme as to prevent the resumption of ordinary, everyday life. What helps the process of grieving to be a healthy one however is the wake, the public funeral.

The funeral and all that surrounds it serves multiple purposes. It enables relatives and friends not merely to mark a death but to celebrate a life. It helps the bereaved by reminding him of the place the dead person holds in minds and hearts other than his own. The very energy and activity of the typical Irish funeral can also anaesthetise the bereaved but when the talking and the eating, the singing and the weeping are over, the pain, postponed and numbed, remorselessly returns as this Galway mother of ten children, whose husband died from cancer, eloquently describes in the course of a radio interview:

> There's a great high to a funeral. There's an awful lot of people about, friends, neighbours. There's a lot of activity to a funeral, but when the funeral is all over everyone goes their own way and that's when it hits you ... I'm here on my own now and I've got to do my own thing.

'You don't have time to grieve', remarks the father of a murdered eighteen year-old regarding the fast-moving conveyor belt that is the classic funeral. Everybody is kind, considerate, and everybody is there for the few days around a death. There are relatives to help with the cooking, friends and neighbours to help with the kids. There is a constant stream of people, familiar and strange, to press your hand and commiserate for 'your trouble' and say something generous and fitting about the deceased. And then there is a kind of silence as people drift slowly back to their own lives and preoccupations, to so-called 'ordinary' life and the gap, the void, the absence, concealed by all the funeral activity, become palpable once more.

AND SO, THE FUNERAL meats cold, the music stilled and the well-wishers gone, the bereaved person enters the *second stage* of normal bereavement. In this stage the person sleeps badly, weeps often uncontrollably, eats poorly and finds it hard to have the zest required for normal living. There is often an intense restlessness and a difficulty both concentrating and remembering.

Many bereaved people now begin to feel guilty about failures to do enough for the deceased while some feel angry and irritable about others. There is real physical discomfort.

The physical pain can be well-nigh unbearable. Not for nothing do we speak of heartbreak. For some time the bereaved can feel in the grip of mental instability – experiencing intense anxiety, unable to concentrate, feel alive, take note of their surroundings. There can be crippling panic attacks, distressing insomnia. None of this betokens mental instability. It is our very essence coming to terms with loss.

Many bereaved individuals have the experience at some time that they are in the presence of the dead person and about ten per cent report brief hallucinations – seeing the dead person, hearing footsteps, sensing his presence. Common too is the temporary forgetting that the person is dead – well described by a widow in her forties whose husband died from cancer, leaving her with three children:

> Often I found I was taking two pieces of meat out of the freezer. I'd say 'I'll do a piece of steak for him tomorrow' or 'we'll have chops for dinner' ... Even buying the food, doing the shopping, I would tend to pick up something and I'd be down two or three aisles in the supermarket and I'd say 'Dear God, what am I doing?' ... for example, Worcestershire sauce was something Noel used that no one else used, and at one stage I went to the press and discovered I had three bottles of it ... I'd buy it, not so much forgetting, but it was such a pattern to my life.

Death indeed ruptures the patterns of survivors' lives. And during this stage, many a bereaved person feels they are losing their mind, they are having a nervous breakdown, going mad. Such is the priority placed on reason and control in our society that bereaved people feel ashamed of feeling, feel embarrassed at losing control, feel enormous social pressure to 'pull themselves together'.

In some cultures, extreme displays of grief are not merely tolerated but are encouraged. Not so in our own. A seemly display of controlled grief is permitted. Excess emotional outpourings are somewhat suspect. And yet there is evidence that the full ventilation of grief is good for one, physically and emotionally. Often people have to be encouraged to let go. A lifetime of keeping emotions under strict check is not easily forsaken in a moment, even in a moment of agonising loss.

IN THE *THIRD STAGE* of normal mourning, these various symptoms slowly abate. Gradually, the bereaved person comes to terms with the new situation. Yet it is important to recognise that no one who has lost someone very close and very dear to them ever is the same again. One should beware of and resist the all too prevalent temptation to rush in and reassure the bereaved that all things must pass, that he or she will 'get over it' and that time is a great healer. Doubtless such reassurance is well-meant but it does miss the point somewhat.

In one very definite sense we never 'get over' death. Death like any great wound leaves a scar. It may heal and the pain may ease but the mark is always there. In over twenty years of interviewing people about their experiences, motives, relationships, I have continually been struck by how death, particularly death of a child, retains an extraordinary potent freshness, timelessness. No matter how many years pass memories and emotions can be summoned up by nothing more substantial than a snatch of a melody or the sight of a child's toy.

The process of normal mourning requires that the bereaved ultimately regain control of their feelings and behaviour so as to permit them to begin again the process of living. But all of us when bereaved will still feel grief and sadness from time to time and in predictable and unpredictable circumstances. The father of that eighteen year-old girl savagely murdered finds the freshness of the memories of her reassuring:

> There's not a day that goes by that I don't think of my daughter. There's not a day that her name is not brought up at home. We talk about Jill, we can drop Jill into conversation about anything. And that's one of the safety valves that we have, that we can speak about her so freely.

If death *for* a child poses a profound challenge concerning the nature of separation and loss, the death *of* a child cries in the face of nature. The mother of Glenn, a little boy who died of cancer, expresses it poignantly:

> I think when your parents go, and you're grown up, or when a brother or a sister goes, that's one thing. But your own child, I mean it defies all the laws. You don't lose your children. You never think you are going to bury them. Nobody expects to be burying their child and I think it is the hardest thing that anyone ever has to do.

DEATH, LIKE LIFE, IS unfair. Some people are given a warning that a loved one is about to die. They are prepared. They can say all those words of love they want to say rather than have to see them written in an obituary that their loved one will never read. The death-bed scene, so beloved of Victorian and opera librettists, has its own comfort but many people in the late twentieth century die sudden, unexpected deaths, leaving the bereaved literally speechless. A woman whose mother died in her sixties from that twentieth century killer, cancer, describes the relief that such forewarning provides in the midst of grief:

> My father and I talked about this ... I said we are so lucky that we are given this opportunity to say all those things to my mother. Had she died suddenly we could never have told her we loved her, never told her about this and that ... and it was a God-given opportunity to say all the things you want to say and never do. The opportunity was marvellous and we did make use of it.

Ours is a culture that has been accused of being evasive in the face of death. We use pallid euphemisms for death itself. People don't die, they 'pass on', 'go to their Maker', 'are at perpetual rest'. Until recently many doctors were more than reluctant even to raise the issue of impending death with patients suffering from potentially terminal illnesses. In truth, it is never an easy question. It is perhaps hardest when the dying person is a child. The parents of a child dying from spina bifida, who brought him from hospital to die at home, talked and cried together and shared their terrible grief. His mother describes her little boy's awareness thus:

> He asked me one day was he going to die. I told him 'no'. I couldn't tell him. And he got to the stage where he always wanted to sit on my lap and tell me he loved me. There were days I knew I couldn't break down in front of him ... I had to keep going. And he'd still be joking, he'd still be laughing. But I think he knew. I do now think he knew.

FOR MANY PEOPLE, A religious faith can provide enormous sustenance in coping with the finality of death. At the end of one of the most moving interviews I ever conducted, the tennis player Arthur Ashe, later to die tragically of AIDS contracted through contaminated blood which he received in the course of heart surgery, described how his great hope was that he would one day be reunited with his beloved mother who died when he was only six years old. 'The boy in me, the little boy in me,' he remarked, 'wonders if I will see my mother again if I die – that makes the spectre of dying more palatable.'

For Ashe, as for many adults who lose a parent when they are themselves young, the personal sense of death was always intense. Ashe admitted to being fascinated by cemeteries and morgues. Of course, however engrossed we may be in our daily activities, there lurks, as Robert Kastenbaum and Ruth Aisenberg observe in their remarkable book *The Psychology of Death* (Duckworth, London, 1974), 'somewhere within us, ready for arousal, a complex of attitudes and anxieties based on the realisation that any hour of any day could be doomsday.' Many of us cope with bereavement and our sense of our own mortality. Religious belief can provide significant comfort, as a young woman who lost her baby through stillbirth movingly describes:

I took some comfort from the fact that there is such a place as Heaven. We believe there is such a place. And we believe she is there. She did nothing, so why shouldn't she be in Heaven? ... A priest called afterwards to see me and I cross-examined him toughly that day as to why God took my baby ... and if God is a just God, why did he take my baby? And the answer he gave was that God took my baby because he needed innocent souls. So I have hung on to the fact that my baby was one of the innocent souls that he needed.

But religious belief is not always reassuring. The God who gives life and takes it away can himself become, for a while, the target of all the pain, the anguish, the anger, the resentment provoked by death. A woman in her early sixties, whose husband is in his seventies and dying from Alzheimer's disease, gives vent to her frustration and bitterness with a fierce passion:

I've blamed God. I've blamed everybody. I've blamed myself. I've blamed my relations. I've blamed God countless times. I've fallen out with God, I've fallen back in with God. I go to Mass and sometimes I don't even say a prayer. I'm in the church and I'm just thinking of Paddy. I just cannot get Paddy out of my mind. He'll never get out of my mind, he'll always be there.

MANY BEREAVED FIND SLEEP-FILLED nights and contentment through visits to the graves of their lost, loved ones. The public cemetery has, over the past one hundred and fifty years, become the focus of all the piety for the dead. Early in the last century, it had become a place to go in order to remember, pray, meditate and mourn. Tombs constructed like little chapels, graves adorned with pious objects, crosses, candles, souvenirs of Lourdes, headstones decorated with pathetic epitaphs, are all readily seen in every graveyard and cemetery in the country, testifying to the potency of the cemetery as the focal point of an assimilation of the living to their dead.

The cemetery binding the living and the dead is an image which recurs throughout literature. In Bronte's great romantic novel, Edgar Linton visits the grave of his dead wife, Cathy, every day and there 'He remembered her, he recalled her memory with a passionate and tender love, full of hope, he aspired to that better world where, he had no doubt, she had gone'. In one of the greatest short stories ever written, James Joyce's *The Dead*, the young and long dead Michael Furey buried at Oughterard comes many years later between the living Gretta and Gabriel Conroy, the story ending with the image of snow lying 'thickly drifted on the crooked crosses and headstones, on the spears of the little gate, on the barren thorns' of the cemetery.

Again and again, in contemporary discussions about death and mourning, the central theme of the grave and the cemetery linking living and dead, reverberates. Here again is the father of the murdered eighteen year-old speaking of his ritual and regular visits to where she lies buried – and his identification of the actual grave with the body buried within is eloquent in its explicitness:

> I visit the grave every week, Saturday and Sunday. I drop over Saturday morning, go up, say a few prayers, come back, light a candle ... We keep the grave nice because we always like to keep her pretty – that's what we say – and she is always pretty with lovely flowers on her grave.

VISITING THE CEMETERY, TENDING the grave, communing with the dead loved one – these are complex, potent psychological and spiritual rituals which contemporary secular western culture tends to decry and consequently pays the price of abnormal reactions, truncated mourning and delayed, distorted grieving. Again and again, simple, ordinary, unsophisticated people when asked testify to the enormous sense of rightness, of peace and of fulfilment that visiting the grave can and does provide. It is summed up by the mother of the little boy, Glenn, who died of cancer, when asked how she continues to keep contact with her beloved child, replied:

I go to the grave every day. It's only five or ten minutes in the car and it's a major part of my life. Everyone has their own point of view, and everyone goes when they want to themselves. If Glenn was here I'd be running after him all day, I'd be cooking for him, playing with him, or doing for him whatever you do for children. So for me to drive five or ten minutes down the road to spend a couple of minutes at the grave – it's doing something for him still.

DEATH OF A SPOUSE

AIDEEN O'KEEFFE

THE DEATH OF A loved partner is one of the worst losses that we can experience. We spend time and effort building up a relationship with another person, settle down to living together and adjust and form new patterns together. We become a workable interdependent unit, each bringing personal qualities and practical skills to help the other and to provide a refuge against the world. Then suddenly it ends – one partner dies and the other is bereft. How can the bereaved partner cope with such a loss? What effects are they likely to experience before picking up their lives again and finding new purpose?

The immediate reaction is one of numbness – no matter what the warning signs were, the finality of death is too shattering to take in immediately and the mind closes up. There is a feeling of disbelief, that the person is in a bad dream and will wake up and find everything is all right again. The presence of family and friends, although comforting, seems to emphasise the dreamlike quality of what is happening. Other people organise the funeral, and the sense of shock brings a strange feeling that the funeral will bring the partner back again. Sometimes, reality does not impinge until the bereaved spouse witnesses the burial and then the stark truth begins to dawn.

NUMBNESS GIVES WAY TO an intense flood of feelings, and anxiety and panic predominate as grief begins. Ordinary routines of everyday life are affected as the spouse's absence becomes obvious. Common physical symptoms are loss of appetite, disturbed sleep and nightmares. The world becomes a threatening place without the life partner and seems darker and more disturbing. Stress causes high arousal in people and produces feelings of alarm, and bereavement is a major stressor to all of us. The spouse may talk repeatedly about the dead partner and fret about all the details of the final illness. They may worry unduly about missed symptoms and experience guilt feelings – 'If only I'd listened to her earlier', or 'If only I'd insisted that he went to the doctor'. Going to bed becomes fearful as all these thoughts prevent sleep and go round and round like a gramophone record. Sleep can bring release for a while and even pleasant dreams of the dead partner, and everything can seem all right again. Then waking brings the cruel realisation that the spouse is dead and the world of surviving without them is back again. Such disappointments can be overwhelming and the simple acts of getting out of bed and getting dressed can seem too daunting.

Taking to bed while experiencing stress and grief can be a very normal primitive response to pain. It coincides with a loss of interest in the outside world and, indeed, the bereaved spouse may be upset to think that the world outside carries on after such a personal catastrophe. The sound of music or laughter may seem disrespectful to the dead partner, and most people who attend to the bereaved spouse tend to speak in hushed tones.

THE ANXIOUS PHASE IS often followed by, or interspersed with, feelings of anger which can be upsetting for other people. The anger can be directed at hospital staff, particularly doctors and nurses, for not saving the partner. It is part of the attempt to make sense of what has happened, to find a reason why the partner died, as death seems to demolish the foundations of what life is about. To look for a mistake in the diagnosis or the treatment seems more acceptable than to believe that life is finite or that the surviving spouse may have overlooked early signs of the illness. Anger can also be a protest to the deceased for dying first, leaving the partner lost and abandoned.

Generalised irritability may be directed at family and friends, and this can be divisive and create lasting friction with in-laws, especially. The surviving spouse may then have to deal with further tensions and injured feelings in the wake of their overwhelming loss.

Bowlby's theories have shown us that it is in the nature of human beings, as well as animals, to form attachments to key figures for physical and emotional survival.[1] The first attachments are to parents, and to mother in particular, and later to chosen partners for shared existence and mutual benefit. The absence of the deceased spouse produces anxiety and pining and the natural solution is to 'search' for the missing partner. This is the stage when restlessness is most evident, as the surviving spouse seeks to 'find' the lost person.

The spouse goes out to look for the partner, but is hardly out when they want to come home again, where the partner normally would be. It is common, during this time, to mistake other people for the deceased spouse or to believe that they heard the partner coming in the door, as usual. This 'searching' behaviour can be fruitful, and some of the pain can be assuaged by the feeling that the deceased spouse is nearby and that their presence can be sensed. This can comfort the bereaved partner by conveying a spiritual belief in the continuing presence of the 'lost' spouse in some afterlife, from where the surviving spouse will be taken care of and watched over.

THE FIRST YEAR OF bereavement is a painful time of dealing with the daily reminders of the shared life, habits and patterns that the couple had built together and which now must be dismantled. The rituals of setting places at the table and preparing meals for two have to be relinquished. Some people find this easier to do on a gradual basis, rather than face the stark reminder of the table for one. All the little things the bereaved person meets each day can be a trigger for acute pangs of grief – for example, the favourite television programme, the newspaper, the shopping rituals. It is important to cry and express emotions during this difficult time. Access to close friends or family members, who will

---

1. Bowlby, John, *Attachment and Loss*, Tavistock Publications, London, 1969; Penguin Paperbacks, Middlesex, 1980.

listen and allow the bereaved person to talk about all these aspects, is very necessary during this first year.

One of the difficulties, in the twentieth century, is the reduced number of mourning rituals, so that people sometimes fade away after the funeral is over. In earlier times, the custom of wearing black clothes or arm bands for at least six months was a useful way of alerting the world to the need to treat the bereaved person gently and to offer help. Studies on bereavement have theorised that improved healthcare this century has removed our awareness of death as a natural part of life. In the nineteenth century, for example, child mortality was high, and appropriate rituals were established to acknowledge death. We seem to have protected society from thinking about death by abolishing these signs of mourning. Sometimes there can be social approval for the person who seems to cope bravely at the spouse's funeral without shedding a tear. After President Kennedy was shot in Dallas, some of us remember how Jacqueline Kennedy was admired for her calm behaviour at his funeral. Far from being a model to follow, such composure only delays grief or represses it to cause problems later.

TO TALK ABOUT THE dead partner as if they were perfect is a common psychological need in the immediate aftermath of death. It helps the spouse to cope with the shock of what has happened and to make sense of the months of caring for the deceased partner in their final illness. In many cases, the surviving spouse was given information regarding the terminal nature of the illness which they then hid from the sick person. This involved a continuous strain in trying to look and sound cheerful when visiting the hospital or looking after the spouse at home.

The idealisation of the deceased, for a time, is a way of dealing with loss and a justification of all the care and time that the survivor spent during the illness. 'He was the best husband anyone could have', 'She was a marvellous wife – there was no one like her'. This gradually passes, some months later, to a more realistic picture of the positive and negative sides of the deceased partner. In some ambivalent relationships, where the surviving partner may have wished the spouse dead at times, there may be lingering guilt and anger, and idealisation and mourning may be protracted.

The early stages of bereavement may be particularly difficult if the partner dies suddenly or when young or middle-aged, when death is not usually anticipated. The numbness phase lasts longer than usual, and family and friends are needed to help with the daily practical tasks and to make any decisions needed, which all bereaved people find difficult.

To take on the identification of the dead partner may be one way of bridging the chasm caused by unexpected death – so the surviving spouse may take up a cause, a hobby or a business which the deceased partner was involved with. By 'carrying the flag' of the lost partner the bereaved spouse feels as if they still 'live on', thus ensuring that their life made some sense and is not forgotten.

ALTHOUGH CHILDREN CAN BE a great source of comfort and continuity later on, studies have shown that they can be an added pressure for a grieving spouse in the early stages of bereavement. The younger they are the more daily attention they need, just at the time when the surviving spouse is shocked and unable to function. Friends, family and neighbours can be of great help in offering to care for children at this stage. Another factor is that children are upset at the loss of their mother or father, and the surviving parent cannot give in to their own grief if required to attend to a distressed child.

Older children, in their teens or twenties, are shattered by their first real encounter with death and the loss of an important figure in their lives, and are not in a position to offer support to the surviving parent. An added pressure for children can be ill-advised words from family friends – for example, 'You'll have to take your mother's place and look after the younger ones', or 'You're the man of the family now, you mustn't cry'.

The surviving spouse and children are faced with the difficult task of regrouping themselves as a family and learning to live without the deceased spouse. It takes time to get the delicate balance adjusted and is often only achieved through trial and error and hurt and angry feelings on all sides.

ONE OF THE MOST painful aspects of the first year of bereavement is the occurrence of key anniversaries, without the deceased partner being there to share them. The first birthday of either spouse, the first bank holiday, the first Christmas and New Year, and especially the first wedding anniversary, are times of fresh pangs of grief for the surviving partner. Memories of happier times come flooding back and the torment can seem unbearable. To the grieving spouse the world seems full of couples, and loneliness intensifies. There are also the anniversaries of the dead partner's illness and death to be faced afresh each year, and it may take about five years before these dates can be faced with equanimity.

In addition to the loss of the loved partner and the stress of bereavement, the surviving spouse may have to cope with the further strain of loss of income and loss of status if the main breadwinner dies. At a time of emotional upheaval and hopelessness, there may be major practical problems of feeding and clothing the family to face. Being forced to deal with state welfare systems for the first time can be an added burden for the distressed widow. For some, a change of house may be required if money is very tight, and this can be particularly stressful when so much else has changed. The widower may be faced with finding suitable housekeeping and childcare arrangements and the upheaval of using strangers instead of his caring wife.

In emotional terms, there are important roles that each partner provides for the other which are also lost through death – adult company to talk to, a confidante to share troubles with and a companion for outings and social events. In traditional marriages, where friendships and social life usually stem from the husband's interests, widows may lose the very people they need to see them through the dark days. Other couples tend to drift away as their social system provides no place for the widow on her own.

There is often, also, a loss of practical skills in the household through death, e.g. cooking, housekeeping, child rearing, home maintenance, gardening, car driving, money management and social organising.

IT IS CLEAR FROM the sections already covered that the death of a spouse is a major loss for any person to deal with. We all know people who never seem to recover, while others pick up the threads of their lives again and gradually blossom in a new way. What factors influence these different responses?

Broadly speaking, previous life experiences and the previous self-esteem of the surviving spouse are the main determinants of bereavement response to a partner's death. So the person who has suffered loss in childhood, particularly of a parent, will be more vulnerable to losing a partner. Similarly, the person whose self-esteem was low before marriage may have enjoyed the shelter of the married state and may have felt affirmed by their partner. The loss of that person may bring back all the old fears about self-worth and they may experience the loss of status as crippling. Bereavement counselling can be very helpful in the above circumstances.

Other factors which affect response are the occurrences of other crises within a two-year period, either before or after the bereavement. For example, the surviving spouse may have had a personal or family illness or may still be grieving the death of a parent. Disharmony with other family members, perhaps through the deaths experienced, may also be a stressor. If the spouse was ill for some time, the bereaved person may feel the loss of the caring role. It is human nature to like to feel needed.

The style of relationship with the deceased partner will influence the survival responses. In traditional marriages, women may have invested a large part of their lives in the relationship and may have become very dependent on their partner. Bereavement will require more substantial adjustments for them, unlike the newer symmetrical marriages where both partners have careers and a circle of contacts outside the marriage.

BY THE SECOND YEAR of bereavement, most surviving spouses experience a return of energy and a gradual renewal of interest in life. Although they experience grief pangs, these are now more episodic. People can begin to talk of their marriage in the past tense and to make some new choices for themselves. This does not mean that the partner is forgotten but rather that they can be viewed as having 'gone before', from where they can be a source of comfort in enabling the surviving spouse to get on with life. Sorting out, and disposing of, the deceased partner's clothes is often seen as a turning-point in this process.

Making new choices can include:

1) Redecorating the house.
2) Planning a holiday with other people, which may be the first venture away without the deceased spouse.
3) Taking care of oneself and one's needs – eating well, and choosing whether to talk to others or to have a quiet time alone.
4) Looking after health needs and taking regular exercise.
5) Asking for help from friends when help is needed. This is essential after the first few months of bereavement, as people often want to help but don't know what is required and keep away out of delicacy.
6) Reviving old hobbies or taking up new ones. Although this may feel stressful at first, sharing an activity with other people builds up a network of acquaintances from which new friendships are formed. The advantage of hobbies like bridge, golf, tennis, arts and crafts, or bowls is that a spouse is not needed and partnerships or teams are formed from club members of both sexes.
7) Training for a new career, if this is required, or seeking employment opportunities from skills already developed in running a home. Age should not be a limiting

factor here, as maturity and life experience are valuable selling points, particularly in service outlets.

8) Voluntary work for those who want to retain some free time. Surviving spouses can make their grief meaningful by offering help to others. There are established bereavement groups like Bethany, which are parish-based, or the National Association of Widows in Ireland, which organises social outings. There are many other organisations, unrelated to bereavement, which are appreciative of voluntary help.

ALTHOUGH IT MAY SOUND strange to prepare for bereavement, there are ways of living which can prevent the worst consequences of grief from occurring. The first two are major emotional issues:

1) Talking through the illness and its implications with the partner. Although this needs to be done very gradually, studies have shown that many patients view this in a positive light. The Hospice system, and Pastoral Care work with terminally-ill people, have helped to address the psychological needs of patients who are in transition from this life to the next. The spouse who can enter into this, by facing the reality of death and sharing fears and deep emotions with the partner, can find this a very meaningful experience. By creating the opportunity to be honest and to listen to what the other partner is feeling, they can enhance the available time left together and make it as beneficial as possible. This helps the sick person on their journey, and also prevents unnecessary guilt feelings afterwards for the bereaved partner.

2) Building up a spiritual belief system which puts life and all its creatures into an interrelated context. It has been found that people with a coherent world-view, based on spiritual values, survive loss more effectively. Religious services and rituals have an important place in validating the life of the deceased and helping the process of adjustment for the bereaved.

The next two guidelines relate to practical preparation:

3) Although there are rewarding and enriching benefits from a relationship with another person, if this partnership is too exclusive it can cause problems. When one dies, the resulting aftermath for the other is potentially harmful. Given that death is a reality of the life process, studies have shown that people operate best in social networks where support and friendship are available in an ongoing way. These systems survive despite the death of individual members, and provide continuity for the remaining members.

4) While division of labour may work well in any given partnership, it is important that each spouse knows how to do the work of the other. So, for example, it is important that the woman knows how to drive the car and is familiar with family finances, even if she leaves those tasks to her husband. Equally, it is important that the man knows how to cook and to work the washing machine, even if he leaves those tasks to his wife. While experiencing the shock and emotional trauma of bereavement is no time to try to learn new survival skills.

THE DEATH OF A spouse is a painful loss to bear and grief is a process which takes time to work through. Yet, like all crises, it can provide the opportunity for growth. People can learn to become more independent, to face fears and to realise their potential. By operating on their own again, new ventures can be tried and new relationships can be made. New friendships can offer a different way of thinking and give us a new perspective of ourselves. It is very important to weed out any negative thoughts like 'My life is over now' or 'I'm too old to do that'. History is full of examples of people who began new ventures and successfully took on new lifestyles in every decade of the life-cycle.

DEATH OF A PARENT

PHIL LARKIN

ALL PEOPLE ARE CHILDREN. Whether our parents are living or dead, we are still referred to as their children. For most people, the death of a parent closes a chapter in their lives, one which draws them back to the emotive and reminiscent feelings of childhood. In our early years, parents represent the stability we need to make sense of the world around. They are available to praise our achievements, correct our immature misdeeds, and offer the wisdom of their maturity – requested or otherwise!

Again, for most people, the death of a parent is seen as something which is a facet of adult life. As we attain adult roles, our parents may reinvest in other useful and purposeful tasks, particularly in their new role as grandparents (still offering the wisdom of counsel). For some adult children, the increasing infirmity of their aged parents requires them to adopt a caring role. The ultimate death of the parent may bring feelings of relief as well as a sense of sorrow and loss. The loss may be viewed in terms of the length of life the parent had and that now their death is a 'just reward' or a 'blessing'.

Although one would not wish to detract from the feelings of adult children who lose a parent, this chapter intends to consider the loss of a parent from the perspective of a child. One may consider why we have chosen this particular group. Certainly, research in the field of childhood bereavement leads us to believe that the trauma of parental death in childhood can have profound psychological consequences in adulthood, specifically depression and the inability to form close relationships.

Black (1992) highlights the fact that children are at a

greater risk of a pathological grief reaction than adults.[1] In this sense, 'pathological' refers to grieving which is in some way delayed or distorted. This may account for reports of a five-fold increase in the risk of an adult psychiatric disorder in children who lose a parent. However, research is somewhat inconclusive on this point and I feel it would be wrong to leave the impression that a bereaved child is at risk of psychiatric illness per se. The debate has largely focused on when children are capable of mourning, and that it is their inability to grieve and mourn fully that leads to the psychological problems in later life. I would strongly agree with the belief of William Worden in his book, *Grief Counselling and Grief Therapy*, that we need to think beyond adult perceptions of grief, and find a way of supporting grieving children in a child-centred way.[2] Restricting children within adult models of grieving can create its own problems. We must also remember that children are part and product of a family; their grieving directly affects their surviving parent and siblings, and often when they need parental love most, it may be denied them because of the surviving parent's grief and inability to cope with the situation.

IT WOULD BE TRUE to say that reactions to grief are largely dependent on the intensity of the relationship with the dead person. The bond that we develop with a parent is often so strong that our attempts to separate from it cause personal trauma to both adult and child, as can often be seen in the teenage years. The death of someone as close to us as a parent can be a devastating blow to our feelings of security and safety. The death of a parent, in whom we have placed ultimate trust, and the fear that others may leave and fail to return just as the parent did, may be one factor which affects the ability to form the close relationships in adult life which were mentioned earlier.

1. Dora Black, 'Helping Young People Grieve', in Barbara Ward and Associates, *Exploring Feelings, Loss and Death with the over 11's and Adults*, Good Grief Publishers, Middlesex, 1992.
2. William Worden, *Grief Counselling and Grief Therapy*, Routledge, London, 1991.

Discussing the child's reactions to a parent's death, in itself creates problems; childhood is not a single entity, but a series of changing states of being as we mature from baby to young adult. It can often be a painful as well as pleasurable process, particularly in the teenage years. Working with bereaved children requires ingenuity and adaptability as well as professional skills. It also requires a sound knowledge of the 'cognitive development' of the child, since the child's responses to, and grief at, the loss of the dead parent are directly related to the stage of cognitive development the child has reached. Cognitive development may best be understood if we appreciate that things we take for granted are a matter of learning for the young child. Knowing how to get dressed properly is a good example of this. Children make sense of the world from their interaction with objects and people. Death is a complex issue to discuss even for adults, so it is no wonder that in the past children were often excluded from such things. The child needs to understand abstract concepts such as 'time', 'always and forever', 'now and then', and 'not coming back'. However, young children are designed to assimilate knowledge quickly, and as any adult will tell you, they have an innate ability to pick up all sorts of information which is usually to be repeated at the most inopportune moment for the parent! In a situation where a parent has died, children will sense the distress of those around them and will need to be told what has happened. What is important is that any explanation is appropriate to their stage of development and awareness of the world around them.

THE DEATH OF A parent in childhood is frequently complicated and may encompass many types of death. The dead parent is likely to be young in adult terms and the surviving parent is grieving the untimely loss of a life partner, as well as trying to readjust to the new social role of a single parent. The cause of death itself may well be sudden and tragic, as in a traumatic accident or suicide, or from a protracted illness such as cancer or neurogenic disease. Such complications in death scenarios warrant whole chapters in them-

37

selves. My aim here is to discuss reactions to a parent's death that the younger child, and then the teenager, may face relative to their stage of cognitive development. Finally, I hope to give some advice based on personal experience of how we, as adults, can help children to cope with their loss.

Although I have chosen to consider children in different age-groupings, much of the information applies across all age ranges, and the individuality of the child is a paramount consideration. For convenience, certain topics have been discussed under age-group headings. Naturally, these topics should be considered 'across the board' and applied to the needs of the child of any age.

FROM THE MOMENT OF birth, children are learning about the world around them. Most learning in early life is through experience and parental guidance. New babies are born with innate reflexes necessary for survival, and they have a need for food, comfort, warmth and cuddles, often in that order. It is usually the mother who is perceived as the person best suited to meet these needs.

Thankfully, the death of a mother through birth trauma in the 1990s is rare, though not unheard of. However, the research shows that provided the care is consistent, loving, and the baby's needs are met, they will thrive. The attachment is to the needs and not necessarily to the person. In the tragic event of a parent's death at this stage, the surviving parent, if able, is probably the best person to carry out the care by virtue of the fact that they are most likely to be around and know the baby's routine.

Having said that, babies appear to like consistency in their care, and this needs to be considered if an adult other than the surviving parent is likely to be involved. The process of attachment to the carer develops reasonably quickly in the first few months, and it is important for the baby's well-being that carers are available to offer full-time attention to their needs, rather than an hour here or there which might disrupt the baby.

Naturally, the new baby is unable to comprehend what has happened, but babies do respond to feelings around them. For example, if a parent is anxious , this may reflect in the child being fractious and not settling appropriately. Babies often need extra cuddles and loving to assure them that everything is all right. Tone of voice is extremely important since babies will react to loud or distressed voices. Singing and speaking softly, using music, as well as rocking and patting will help to soothe the baby. The surviving parent may derive comfort from these actions, and they should be enabled to do so. The support of friends with practical experience to assist with daily rituals such as shopping or housework is the best help that can be given at this time. One particular difficulty for babies as they grow is imagining the dead parent whom they have never known, as a real person. As the babies grow up, they will require information about the parent they never knew.

In the age of the video, it is possible to have a visual image of the dead parent which provides a focus for discussion about them. Photographs provide a similar focus. Keeping special mementos from the dead parent's possessions for the child as he grows, will help the child to realise that the dead parent was once a real person, a part of the surviving parent's life, and a part of the child's life story. In the case of a dying parent, a letter is one of the best ways of helping to share the sadness of leaving a child behind. These considerations apply not only to the child with limited knowledge of the parent, but to any child who can refer to them as they get older and their sense of reality develops.

AS THE BABY GROWS, he learns that an object or person may exist even if it is out of sight. From this, the child becomes increasingly aware that objects or persons can be met time and time again, and are still the same object or person but in a different situation. Exactly when a child achieves this is a matter of debate, and anything from six months to three years has been suggested. The importance of this is that when this stage is reached in the child's development, we can see the child increasingly upset and distressed if the parent goes away and does not appear to come back. This is often called 'separation anxiety'. He will look for them and show pleasure when they do return, although if the separation is prolonged, he may act with indifference to the parent or transfer his affections to another carer. What the child is exhibiting is a form of grieving which is related to his feeling of loss and security.

The death of a parent in these early years is most traumatic. By virtue of the fact that the child is becoming more aware, the loss of his carer will be acute and painful. The work of John Bowlby (1980),[3] on bonding and attachment, highlights the toddler's view of the world. Now with a strong attachment to the mother (or mother-figure), any separation is distressing. In the analogy of the supermarket, any toddler who loses his mother amongst the shelves will soon make his presence and unhappiness known to all around. We can imagine, therefore, the level of distress when the attachment is broken because the parent has died. His greatest fear is of being abandoned by the person he has come to trust. This child is still too young to understand the concept of his parent's death, and is usually unable to grasp any idea that death is irreversible and permanent, but can be sorrowful and aware of the sadness around him. The development of language enables him to vocalise his fears, such as 'I want Mummy', although he is unable to put his feelings into words since his vocabulary is limited.

Toddlers and young children have a very egocentric view of life. 'Mine' and 'no' are integral to their small vocabulary. Similar to the baby, the toddler has basic needs to be met, and these will need to be attended to despite the tragedy of the parent's death. This can make the practical arrangements difficult to organise and the mourning by adults and older children more difficult, with a toddler demanding attention. In order to feel secure, ritual is a big part of a toddler's life and reasoning is not a skill the toddler has developed. The death of a parent will not alter his need for meals, bathtime and stories. Again, a friend with practical experience can be a great support to the remaining grieving

3. John Bowlby, *Attachment and Loss* (in three volumes), Penguin Publications, London, 1969, 1973, 1980.

parent. Sometimes, the parent may find it comforting to carry out the routine tasks of childcare, as this allows for a rest from the grief work and enables the toddler and surviving parent to cement their relationship at a time when their security and safety have been threatened. As previously stated, young children sense when something is wrong.

At this age, they find separating fact from fantasy difficult, and may believe that they did something wrong which caused the death. Although their awareness is limited, taking the child away from the scene only leads to bewilderment and confusion, and I would advocate that a child of any age should stay within the family group if at all possible. Removal from the family may only serve to reinforce the misplaced belief that their 'badness' has given rise to the punishment of separation.

DEALING WITH A YOUNG child when one parent is dying can be a heavy burden. However, small children like to be helpful, and this can be utilised. Even the smallest child can bring comfort to the dying parent through their actions. In a family where the mother was dying, I can remember a child of two bringing pillows and handkerchiefs for her mother, as she had seen the nurses do. Although a relative had suggested that this child should be moved to her own house during the mother's final illness, it was deemed more appropriate for the relative to move in with the family and look after the two year-old, who stayed with her mother until just before she died and was able to be a part of the family grief on her death.

The word 'why?' can be most frustrating for any parent. For a young child, it is a first step towards rationalising the reality of what is happening around them. Sometimes, the child may say 'why?' just to enjoy hearing the sound of his own voice. We shouldn't feel we have to answer all the questions all the time. If we think of a parent who is terminally-ill, there is little point discussing the illness or potential outcome in detail with a toddler who has limited language and interpretive skills. However, children can sense dishonesty, and protection from the truth of the matter is unhelpful at any stage. Honesty and simplicity are the key words with all children. Carers should attempt to keep the toddler's world organised and stable despite the trauma.

If we consider the older pre-school child (three to five years), their increasing cognitive abilities bring a greater awareness of death, although it is not seen as a part of their own lives, nor are the concepts of permanence and irreversibility fully understood. Children of this age can show a primitive logic about death, and state clearly and repetitively that 'Daddy is dead', without being aware of the impact of that statement. Adults should not expect 'adult' reactions of tears, distress and sadness. These may come later, and the child may ask about what has happened many times as if not previously told. This can be distressing for the surviving parent, but sharing the sadness enables the child to appreciate that it is all right to be upset. It would also be quite acceptable for a child to return to his play, having been told such news. Play is the child's method of learning about his world; it provides safety and security as well as fantasy. Adults can learn much from a child at play, and certainly play is an excellent mode in which to express feelings through creative or destructive games. Play can open doors to conversation about the death; children are often heard talking to their toys, and it is occasionally helpful to eavesdrop on a conversation which might give some idea of how the child is feeling at that time.

IT IS QUITE COMMON to show traits of regressive behaviour at any age following a parent's death, but particularly so for toddlers and young children at this age. This may be limited to excessive clinginess, hair-pulling, thumb-sucking and bed-wetting. Provided that the child is cared for and nurtured, these behaviours usually pass without complication. Continued problems should be referred for professional help, to reassure the carer that things are all right. At this age, we can begin to prepare children for an awareness of death through teaching them about losses; often the death of an older person or relative, or even a family pet, is an ideal opportunity to introduce the subject.

The child can see that people are sad and that certain rituals are involved, including burial or cremation, bringing flowers, saying prayers, and they may like to be involved in this. The practical nature of the young child's life means that he will welcome being involved in the preparations for the parent's funeral, even if he does not understand the full impact of the day. It is essential that realities such as why we attend a funeral, and why we are buried or cremated are explained *before* the child becomes involved. Attending the funeral is often a contentious issue, particularly if older relatives feel a child's presence is unhealthy. Provided explanations as to the purpose and nature of a funeral have been given, there is no reason why a child should not attend. Funerals give a necessary reality to the events that have taken place and are an essential part of our grieving. Finding the right words can be difficult, but something simple along the lines of the following may be useful: 'Do you remember that Mummy was very sick? Well, Mummy couldn't get better and her body got very tired and then she died. When you die, you don't need your body anymore, you don't need to eat or sleep or breathe. Because you don't need your body, we bury it in the ground in a special place called a cemetery. People will be able to visit Mummy when she is buried, although we cannot see her anymore. We will remember that she was buried there and we can visit that place too. We can take flowers and you can still talk to her and tell her special things if you want. There is no need to be afraid because Mummy made sure that there would be special people, like me, to look after you because she couldn't stay to do that herself. It's all right to be sad and we will take one day at a time ... is there anything you want to ask?'

This short example highlights areas that need to be considered when working with a young child. In particular, the fact that Mummy is no longer present to us is important to get across, as well as the fact that she cannot come back. Similarly, the fact that the child will be cared for needs to be explored, as young children, like their toddler counterparts, fear that their needs will not be met. Always give time for the child to ask questions and answer them as honestly as possible. It is far better to say 'No one knows the answer to that', than to make up a story. Children have long memories! There are many excellent books for children which explain death, covering all different viewpoints, and they can be bought in many bookshops.

THE SCHOOL-AGED CHILD IS nowadays developing a stronger awareness of death, frequently reinforced through the media. By the age of about eight, the finality and irreversibility of death can be appreciated. This varies considerably, but the child of this age has developed a concept of himself which is sufficient to appreciate aspects of living and dying. However, he may not see these issues as having any bearing on his personal life: fantasy is a large part of the life of these children, as can be seen in their enjoyment of cartoons and comics. The concept of 'magical thought' can begin to develop as young as three years of age. One thing often noticeable is the magical thought in playground games that suggests that death is still reversible. 'Bang! Bang! You're dead!' and the child falls to the ground, only to get up again and carry on playing. This is reinforced by fairy stories and the belief in the concept of 'happy ever after'. If working with a child whose parent has died, it is important to help them distinguish between fantasy and reality. As Polombo (1978) has discussed, children between five and nine years are a particularly vulnerable group. They may have developed some understanding, but have very little coping capacity.[4]

This child will still need to know that he is not responsible for anything that may have happened to the parent. Children of this age also have a sense of the macabre – they want to know details about the parent's death, or invent tales of being buried alive. This may lead to nightmares, which are common in this age-group. The child may have a need to reiterate the events of the parent's death and funeral to friends and other adults, largely through play. This is not

4. J. Polombo, 'Parent Loss and Childhood Bereavement'. Paper presented at conference on Children and Death. University of Chicago. In William Worden, *Grief Counselling and Grief Therapy*, Routledge, London, 1991.

abnormal, but the principal carer should be available to correct misinterpretations about the death and funeral.

The child may also exhibit phobias, for example about the dark. Sleep and appetite disturbance are common, as are other somatic complaints, such as headaches, tummy-ache and vague aches and pains. By and large, these should be treated sensitively as they arise. There are some things to be aware of here.

In the case of a sick parent, the child may mimic the symptoms which led to their illness and worry that it may be catching. They may be frightened if they get a cold or ear infection that it might cause them to die or go away like the dead parent; the child is trying to make sense of what has happened, and it is important to reassure the child that he is well, or if sick, that he is going to get better. Most parents would always get things checked out by the GP just in case! Secondly, the desire to be ill (and therefore stay at home) may be a reflection of the child's need to stay close to the surviving parent in case anything should happen to them. Keeping a close eye on the surviving parent reassures them that he or she is not going to go away and leave them. In the case of the surviving parent becoming sick, it is essential that children are reassured as to the health of the surviving parent, and that it is safe to leave them. Children may also show their reaction to the death through compulsive behaviour. There is a need for the child to redefine his safety and security in light of the tragedy of the parent's death.

In order to help him through this time, I would advocate the support of an adult who is not too preoccupied by the loss, as well as the surviving parent. Remember also that even older children deal in the practical realities of life, and issues such as 'Who will pay my allowance now?' and 'Will I have to move house or change school?' are very real to them. Obviously, changes will not occur immediately, but any change should be discussed by the family before it happens if the surviving parent wants to effect a smooth transition.

THERE ARE TWO AREAS that frequently cause concern for families and carers alike. These are 'religious philosophy' and 'schools'. In a predominantly Roman Catholic country such as the Republic of Ireland, it is normal to utilise the belief in an afterlife to explain what has happened to the parent. The idea of a Heaven, where loved ones are happy and content, can be a comforting thought. However, there is no evidence that religious beliefs are consoling to children. Indeed, the abstract nature of the concepts can be frightening. Children deal in realities; the idea of 'Daddy being with the angels in Heaven' does not convey the permanence of death. Heaven could be a country abroad. Any discussion of Heaven and an afterlife must revolve around the important concepts that we believe people are safe and happy, that they cannot come back from Heaven, nor can we visit. Similarly, we often use terms such as 'gone to sleep', 'taken from us', and 'went away to God'. Again, these terms are unhelpful, and clear concise words that convey the idea that people neither wake up nor return from death are important. It is not unheard of for a child who is told about dead parents 'falling asleep', to refuse to go to sleep for fear that they might die too! It is important that death is not seen as a form of punishment or retribution, which again may trigger fantasies in the child's mind. We must also be aware of the children where the family has no particular religious belief, and the fear of 'What happens to my Daddy?' when surrounded by a very Catholic view of death and dying.

A scenario along the following lines may be helpful:

When we die, some people believe that a part of us (our spirit) goes on living in a special happy place we call Heaven. No one knows where Heaven is, or what it looks like, but we believe that Daddy is in this place called Heaven, with God. God is very special because God is all about loving and caring, and so that is what Heaven is, loving and caring. It helps us to think that Daddy is happy when we miss him so much ...

Another issue that can cause a problem is the idea that 'Daddy is watching over you'. The effects of this idea on the imagination of the young child are immense. 'Does Daddy know when I do something naughty?' I have met adults who still bear the scars of having been told that they are under twenty-four hour surveillance. My advice is simple. Do not say it at all!

THE GOLDEN RULE IS always to tell the school. Naturally, the child will need a few days away from school, and there is no set 'period of mourning' in our society. I believe the child should be encouraged, rather than hurried, back to school, in an attempt to regain a sense of normality about the situation. One should bear in mind the child's possible fears of separation from the surviving parent, as mentioned earlier, and these should be addressed before he/she returns to school.

Once back at school, class teachers should be aware of exactly what happened, particularly if the death was in any way traumatic. The teacher will need to prepare the classmates of the bereaved child for what has happened. In Ireland, it is common for classmates to attend the funeral or send messages to their friend. This latter consideration is an excellent way of making the bereaved child feel he is a wanted part of the group.

A disturbing trend, sometimes seen in schools, is that of bereavement bullying. Children can be cruel, and cruelty often stems from their own fear. Incidents of children being taunted for having only one parent, or made to feel different because they may no longer be able to afford to join in school activities due to possible changes in family finances, are not uncommon. This is particularly true if the death has been reported in the media and is therefore assumed to be 'public property'. Teachers need to be sensitive to the bereaved child, particularly when talking about the home situation, inviting parents to parent/teacher meetings, etc. A word of sympathy is also offered to teachers. Having arranged a support-day for schoolteachers on coping with death in a classroom setting, it became all too clear just how unprepared they are for such crises: the workbook by Barbara Ward and Associates, and listed at the end, would be an asset to any teacher's bookshelves. One should also be aware of the stress imposed in the school system by examinations, particularly the Leaving Certificate. I would advocate that children who have been recently bereaved should be given the option of opting out for the year, and repeating when they are in a better frame of mind to study.

THE TEENAGE YEARS ARE often the most difficult in terms of development. Emotions and feelings oscillate between the safe, known world of childhood and the exciting, yet potentially threatening world of being an adult. The death of a parent in the midst of this barrage of fluctuating emotions can be devastating. On the one hand, adolescents can be supportive, caring and able to assist with decision-making; on the other hand, wanting the security and comfort that they received as young children is a very natural response too. There is great variation in developmental progress at this age, and above all, individuality should be respected.

The adult concept of death is formed from about the age of eleven, although as stated, there are wide variations in this. For young adults, death is a concept of personal relevance which can be seen as a continual possibility from birth. This does not imply that the young adult has the ability to analyse feelings, and dealing with the crisis of parental death is as much a trauma for them as for younger siblings. Indeed, older children and adolescents will have identified with their parents as individuals, and recalling the past they have had together may make grief work more poignant. However, the young adult is able to see the effect the death of the parent has had on the family structure, and may be able to provide support to family members.

Tension between young adults and parents is a normal part of growing-up. Arguments are common and can lead to outbursts of temper, sulking and long periods of silence. Parallels can be drawn with the tantrums of the young child, as he explores his new feelings. The death of a parent around the time of one of these arguments can cause a sense of guilt and angst about things that were said unintentionally. This may be particularly the case if the death is sudden and unexpected. In the event of this situation arising, it is essential to get two points across. Firstly, the young person is not responsible for the tragedy that has occurred; nothing that was said or done could have prevented the death. Secondly, they need to know that despite what may have been said or done, they are still loved by the surviving parent, and that the dead parent loved them too. For some, it actually helps for them to say out loud 'I am sorry for what I said – I didn't mean to hurt you'. In this way, they can enable themselves to move on through their sorrow.

It would be true to say that most young people have a greater affinity with one parent than the other. This does not mean that they love one less, but that they find a closer affiliation to one in terms of outlook and expectation. This can lead to feelings of intense grief if the death is of the closer parent. Furthermore, it can lead to disharmony with the surviving parent. For some adolescents, they find a sense of freedom (which is possibly misplaced), believing that they are less likely to be chastised. For others, the surviving parent is seen as a tyrannical dictator, and as the other parent is dead, there is no 'court of appeal'.

Parents often experience anxieties over how to deal with unruly teenagers. Issues such as staying out late and associating with 'the wrong crowd' can become battlefields. In reality, there needs to be a good degree of 'give and take'. Teenagers need to appreciate the extent of the tragedy that faces the surviving parent, and parents need to realise that their children are young adults who need space. Parents are quite within their rights to ask for help and understanding, and to get it. So are teenagers. Older children often derive comfort from friends, and the peer group is an important part of adolescent development. It is also not uncommon to withdraw from friends because they feel different and unable to communicate their feelings. Friends, too, often find it easier to stay away than risk becoming involved. Young adults may choose to express their grief privately, and this should be respected. As Earl A. Grollman states in his book, *Straight Talk about Death for Teenagers*, loneliness and being alone are not the same.[5] Feeling that you want to spend some

5. Earl A. Grollman, *Straight Talk about Death for Teenagers. How to Cope with*

time alone is nothing to be afraid of.

The fact that the young adult may appear unaffected by the tragedy does not mean that they do not need support. Particularly for boys, the fear of rejection by the peer group for appearing 'soft' may lead them to suppress their emotions or seem blasé in the face of their grief. Adolescents need to be given a clear indication that sadness, tears and anger are all perfectly acceptable emotions at this time. Feelings do change over time, and the young person should be encouraged to take time out and consider 'What am I feeling now?' For some people, grief can be disabling, and it is very important to create space and let feelings take a natural course. Having already mentioned life-changes following a parent's death, a big issue that can arise, particularly for the young adult, is the issue of increased responsibility. Often the young person is expected, implicitly or otherwise, to replace the dead parent. Phrases such as being 'the man of the house' are a typical example of this. These misplaced responsibilities are often imposed on younger children as well as adolescents. It is wrong for us to place these responsibilities on the child or young adult. They are, after all, grieving children, and not normally responsible for adult realities, such as keeping a home or raising a family. However, there is no reason why the young adult should not be asked for their help and, where a choice exists, most would be happy to help.

As previously mentioned, changing financial status is a common problem following the parent's death. This can be more so if the father was the only breadwinner. A shortage of money can lead to curtailment of activities, even a need to shelve life-plans such as college or university for the young adult. Again this can lead to friction in the home. Young adults, unlike young children, can be reasoned with, and in the case of lack of money and asking for their help, young people can often appreciate the reality of the situation. This does not make the situation any less sad, only perhaps more bearable. The most important point is to talk about the

Losing Someone You Love, Beacon Press, Boston, 1993.

changes and discuss issues as a family as far as possible.

IN MANY WAYS, THIS chapter has only touched on some of the issues and problems associated with the death of a parent. There is no right or wrong way for children to grieve and their reactions may be many and varied. There are, however, some key points worth remembering:

1) Honesty in all things is essential for children, especially if you want to develop a sense of trust. Involve them in the situation, particularly funeral arrangements.
2) Remember that children can only grieve to the level of their cognitive development. They need rests from grieving, and may 'pick up where they left off' as they progress through childhood.
3) Share your grief and sadness. It shows the child that it is all right to feel sad about their parent's death too.
4) Keep it simple. Be prepared to explain things several times. There are some excellent storybooks that explain death to children.
5) Encourage the child to express feelings through creative play, particularly where language and talking about the death is a problem.
6) Most problems children face are to do with their insecurity and feelings of helplessness and loss of control. Try to offer security and safety and understanding to help them regain some stability in their lives.

DEATH OF A CHILD

DR FIN BREATNACH

AS A RESULT OF the dramatic improvements in healthcare technology over the past few decades, the death of a child is thankfully a comparatively rare event in the western world. However, some children do die. In 1993 in Ireland, there were over 486 deaths among those under fifteen years of age! The impact of death in childhood is out of all proportion to its incidence in terms of the number of people affected by the death and the appalling severity of the effects. Numerous studies have shown that those who have had the misfortune to have lost a spouse, a parent and a child through death, will invariably describe their grief for their child as the most long-lasting, painful and difficult to overcome.

Much of our knowledge of the bereavement process results from studies of bereaved widows, since this group was the easiest population to reach among the bereaved. These early studies gave us an understanding of the normal grief process and began to define the criteria for abnormal or unresolved grief. However, more recent work has shown that for parents, the effects of losing a child are quite unique and unlike any other loss. In addition, we have learned that the traditional concepts used in relation to the death of a spouse cannot be applied to parental bereavement, because many of the criteria used to define abnormal grief in a spouse are commonly seen in the normal process of parental grieving. The loss of a child raises specific issues not found in any other form of bereavement. These very issues may result in the incorrect diagnosis of abnormal grief in bereaved parents, thereby adding to their distress.

We have also learned that no two bereavements are the same, and that each individual's response will be unique. In addition, we have gained an appreciation of the enormous impact that the death of a child can have on all members of the family unit. Each member is affected in a unique way. The reasons for these differences are many and varied. The role of each parent in relation to the dead child will be a major influencing factor. For example, one parent may have spent so much more time with the child than the other, or the dead child may have been the only boy or girl, the youngest, the eldest or their only child.

The age at death of the child may create specific difficulties; death during pregnancy resulting in miscarriage, or death at the time of birth resulting in a stillborn baby, causes underestimated grief for parents who are denied any tangible proof for the outside world of the existence of their child. Death of the child during adolescence, at a time when the parent/child relationship may have been somewhat ambivalent, can often create feelings of guilt and thereby prolong the grieving process. However, the uniqueness of parental grief for their dead child is not determined by the age of the child at the time of death, but rather by the enormous biological deviation from their expectations which the death has caused.

The mode of death is also likely to play a part in determining the severity and duration of the parents' grief. Sudden unexpected death does not allow for any preparation for the death, and if caused by an accident, may be accompanied by appalling disfigurement. Death by murder is particularly horrific and is frequently associated with prolonged grieving. Emotional problems in parents are common following such deaths, as the parents frequently feel that they have somehow failed their child by not protecting it from harm. Although death following a prolonged, chronic or painful illness will usually have allowed some time for preparation, such an illness may well have drained the resources of the family long before the death and may even have caused its destruction.

The response of each bereaved sibling may also show enormous variation. The dead child may have been a best friend, the only brother or sister, a confidant, the eldest or youngest or a twin. The death, particularly when preceded by a prolonged illness which is commonly accompanied by some over-indulgence of the ill child, may cause feelings of remorse and guilt in surviving siblings, who greatly resented the special attention which the child had received. Adding to their difficulties are the problems created by the traditional outpouring of sympathy for the parents following their loss, with little attention being paid to the needs of the siblings. These siblings have come to be called the 'forgotten mourners'. In an effort to 'protect' the siblings, parents may be reluctant to display their grief, giving rise to fears in the siblings that they would not be mourned either if they were to die. It must always be remembered that these children will almost certainly live longer with the loss than anyone else. In addition, the death of the child awakens in the siblings fears concerning the reality of their own eventual death.

The effects on grandparents following the loss of a grandchild have received scant attention from researchers over the years and without doubt have been underestimated. As it is common nowadays for both parents to work outside the home, frequently one of the grandparents is the main giver of care to the child during working hours. For such grandparents, their grief reaction may be as intense and painful an experience as it is for the parents. In addition, as well as suffering the loss of a loved grandchild, these grandparents also have to endure the heartache which their own child is suffering together with feelings of guilt at having outlived their grandchild!

GIVEN THAT AS MUCH as 20 per cent of all confirmed pregnancies end in miscarriage or spontaneous abortion, this form of death accounts for more deaths than any other cause in childhood. Despite its frequency, the significance of loss through miscarriage is frequently minimised. Often the assumption is made that, since the baby was never born, its parents have nothing to grieve. What we fail to recognise here is that the parents, especially the mother, have already developed a relationship with the unborn child from the moment that the pregnancy was confirmed. The significance of the pregnancy and the mother's relationship to her unborn child develop at an earlier stage than for fathers. The bodily changes which the mother experiences reinforce this attachment. In many instances, the severity of the grief varies between the mother and the father, with the father recovering from the experience far sooner than the mother. Occasionally, however, fathers will bond with the unborn child at an early stage in pregnancy and, for these, their grief will be much like that of the mother's.

The degree and severity of grief which parents suffer following a miscarriage is not determined by the length of time between conception and the miscarriage, but by the significance which the pregnancy held for the parents. If the significance of the parents' loss goes unrecognised, then the normal grieving process cannot take place and the couple are more likely to suffer the destructive consequences of unresolved grief.

We have to understand that for many parents who have lost a child through miscarriage, guilt and self-blame are issues that require resolution. They require adequate explanation as to the possible causes for the miscarriage and reassurance that it was not caused by any act of commission or omission on their parts. The loss can be significantly painful for parents who have experienced difficulties in achieving pregnancy. For them, the loss may produce extreme anxiety about their ability to ever have children of their own. Mothers, in particular, frequently struggle with feelings of worthlessness or with a sense of failure at being unable to produce a healthy child.

To help these parents recover from their loss it is important that the loss be recognised. The family and close friends of such parents should be encouraged to offer their support. Frequently, the mothers are in receipt of much sympathy, with little recognition given to the loss experienced by the father. As the miscarriage often takes place in a hospital setting, it is essential that these institutions provide a private area where parents are allowed to express their sense of loss. In addition, it should be mandatory that follow-up bereavement counselling be offered by the medical and nursing staff in these institutions. It is common in many hospitals for the miscarried baby to be photographed. While many parents treasure the photograph and preserve it as proof that their child existed, all parents should be given the opportunity of seeing the baby also, even if the baby suffers from a significant malformation. Parents cope remarkably well with this situation and frequently concentrate on all that is normal rather than abnormal in their baby.

These measures provide the parents with confirmation that their loss is recognised and facilitate the grieving process, thereby reducing the risk of mental ill-health in the future. These and all the other parents who have lost a child through death, should be given ample opportunity to discuss the available options concerning funeral arrangements. Although baptism is not offered to babies who miscarry, as this is a sacrament for the living, the Church's more enlightened attitude in the recent past has resulted in the death of these babies being recognised through the naming of the baby and the provision of a funeral service.

UNLIKE DEATH THROUGH MISCARRIAGE, the death of the stillborn infant is anticipated prior to birth. For the mother, the first signs are of an absence of the movements of her baby which she had become accustomed to for a number of months. The ultrasound soon confirms the absence of life in her baby. This is a most traumatic time for the parents, and in the midst of their raw emotions they have to decide whether or not the pregnancy should be allowed to continue until natural labour occurs or whether labour should be induced. As all parents almost invariably wish to see and hold their babies, it is important that they understand that if they wait for natural labour to deliver their dead baby, maceration (deterioration of the dead baby's body) will occur. In contrast, induction of labour will produce a baby whose appearance is more likely to meet the expectation of its parents and extended family.

Once the stillborn infant has been delivered, parents

should be given an opportunity to see and hold the baby. Anger is frequently encountered with parents sometimes blaming the doctors, nurses, the hospital or even each other. It is extremely important for all parents to receive an adequate explanation as to the probable cause of death of their baby. A post-mortem examination is frequently requested so that an exact cause of death might be determined. Self-blame, particularly on the part of mothers, is not infrequent. A mother may feel that the death was caused by something which she did or did not do during her pregnancy. If she had resented the loss of freedom which her pregnancy had caused, she may feel extremely guilty at her loss and feel that she is being punished in some way.

As with parents who have suffered a miscarriage, parents who have experienced a stillbirth are often quite young and may have had no previous experience of death. Many parents find reading material on perinatal death and grief both helpful and reassuring and they should always be offered this and encouraged to take such literature home with them. All the options open to these parents in relation to the funeral must be carefully and sympathetically explained. The effects of the death on the siblings must not be minimised. Frequently, young children are extremely excited at the prospect of having a new baby at home. They require an explanation from their parents and from caregivers as to why the baby died. These siblings must be reassured that the baby's death could not have been caused by any action or thought on their part. The word 'death' *should* be used and euphemisms such as 'Too good for this world', 'Taken from us' or 'Gone to sleep' should be avoided for obvious reasons. Experience has taught us that it is important that these children be given an opportunity of becoming involved in the funeral arrangements. Not only do they appreciate the opportunity of saying goodbye in their own way, but such involvement assists the normal grieving process.

NEWBORN OR NEONATAL DEATH refers to death occurring in the first twenty-eight days of life. The causes of newborn death are common to miscarriage and stillbirth – for example, abnormal development within the womb, premature delivery and complications occurring during labour. With extreme prematurity, the baby may be born without the capacity to survive as a result of immaturity of vital organs, particularly the lungs. Alternatively, there may be unexpected problems during labour which can fatally damage an otherwise healthy baby.

Approximately one half of all newborn deaths occur within the first three days of life. Unfortunately, at this time, many mothers may still be confined to obstetric departments and their seriously-ill baby may well have been transferred to a specialised intensive-care unit some distance away. This separation of mother and child prevents the bonding which is so essential to their relationship. The fathers of such babies are torn between their wish to see their ill child and their wife's need for comfort and support. It is essential, therefore, for the medical and nursing staff in the intensive care unit to give parents an accurate day by day account of their baby's condition and of the attempts being made to save the child's life. The parents, of course, should be offered the opportunity of visiting the baby in the intensive-care unit, and open access for parents and siblings should be encouraged. Before seeing the baby the family should be fully-informed about what to expect. These babies require the most sophisticated technology to offer them a chance of life, but this means that, if unprepared, the parents' first sight of their child can be quite a frightening and distressing experience with their baby attached to and apparently enveloped by many tubes, wires and bleeping machines. Parents need to know that everything that can be done is being done. They will derive some consolation from this knowledge.

Parents will usually have an intense longing to hold the baby and they may well be frustrated in this because of the baby's ill-health. The nursing staff should encourage the parents to hold their babies whenever possible and to assist in their babies' care. However, particularly if the prognosis for their baby is extremely poor, many parents may withdraw physically and emotionally from the baby in anticipation of its death. This reaction can produce feelings of guilt later on which can be most distressing to parents. When a newborn twin is dying this can create special difficulties for parents, with their energy split between the two babies.

Unlike death from miscarriage and stillbirth, newborn death by definition means that the baby had an independent life for some time. Parents greatly value that life, however limited, and will speak in terms of hours and minutes rather than weeks or months when describing their loss. In common with miscarriage and stillbirth, those parents who have lost a newborn child have a burning desire to know what happened, why it happened and whether anything else could have been done. It may be vital to perform a post-mortem examination if it is felt that anything further can be learnt which might help the parents in their grief. Regardless of whether or not a post-mortem is performed, all parents and family members should be invited back to the hospital for a follow-up meeting so that any unanswered questions can be aired. The baby's brief life can be reviewed at such a meeting and the care offered in attempting to prevent its death can be outlined. Siblings should be offered an opportunity to ask questions also and to have any concerns addressed. The findings of the post-mortem examination, if performed, should be carefully and sympathetically explained. Future pregnancies can be discussed and, if necessary, genetic counselling can be arranged.

MORE HAS BEEN WRITTEN in the medical literature on Sudden Infant Death Syndrome (SIDS) than on any other form of death in childhood and yet, although the term sounds precise and definite, the causes of SIDS have yet to be defined. By definition, SIDS refers to the sudden death of an infant which is unexpected and despite a full post-mortem examination, an adequate cause of death is not determined. The incidence of SIDS in Ireland has been reduced dramatically as a result of recent research. Parents are now

59

advised that babies should sleep on their side or on their back rather than on their front. Overheating of their babies through the use of too many blankets or clothing should also be avoided. Nevertheless, despite taking these precautions, we have no way of predicting or preventing a SIDS. In some of the babies, the death is preceded by a minor illness such as a common cold, but more often the babies are noted to be entirely healthy prior to death. The death occurs very suddenly, usually during sleep and there is no evidence of struggling or of suffering. It is most important to reassure parents that SIDS is not an hereditary condition and there is no greater chance of it occurring in one family than another.

What is particularly traumatic for SIDS parents is the sudden and unexpected nature of the death. There is no opportunity whatsoever to prepare for it and no chance to say goodbye. Unlike death following a prolonged illness, there is no opportunity to come to terms with the reality of the loss with time. The experience is totally overwhelming for them and almost defies description. Their baby had survived the hazards of pregnancy and the trauma of labour and delivery, and was in every way a healthy baby. They had begun to relax a little and to allow themselves the pleasure of fantasising about the wonderful future which lay ahead for their child. And now their dreams had been completely and utterly shattered. How could such a healthy child, who had been feeding well, been active and responsive, be dead? Surely the death could have been prevented? The traumatic nature of the parents' grief is so powerful and overwhelming that it may prevent them from functioning and destroy their self-confidence.

The absence of a definite cause of death increases the likelihood of parents experiencing guilt reactions. This is often fed through criticism or unhelpful comments by family and friends which can create further doubts in the parents' minds. The involvement of the police, which is a legal requirement, further compounds their difficulties. Similarly, siblings may also have to struggle with feelings of guilt as a result of the ambivalent feelings which they may have had towards their new sibling. In addition, siblings have to cope with their bereavement without the support of their grieving parents who have little energy left to deal with the needs of the children.

Lack of sensitivity on the part of professionals and the public may prolong the grief for parents of a SIDS death. The significance of the loss may be minimised in view of the shortness of the child's life. Telling parents that they are young enough to have other children or that they are lucky that they have an 'angel in Heaven' can be particularly insensitive and tend to invalidate the family's loss. It is essential that these parents be allowed access to medical professionals in order that their many questions relating to the unexpected death of their child can be addressed. They require an explanation of our current understanding of SIDS death and an opportunity to have information repeated and clarified until they are satisfied. We must be aware that, as SIDS is such a topical issue, new theories are frequently reported in the press which force these parents to relive the nightmare again and again. Involvement with the Irish Sudden Infant Death Association may be particularly helpful for many bereaved parents who, through such associations, discover that they are not alone.

WHETHER A CHILD DIES suddenly or following a prolonged illness, the loss felt by its parents and family would be felt just as deeply. However, studies of families following sudden death have reported much more intense and prolonged grieving amongst those who have lost a child suddenly. Parents are immediately thrown into a state of shock. This shock will manifest itself in a number of ways: uncontrolled shaking, weeping, dryness of the mouth and throat, confusion, weakness and intensive feelings of unreality. Such parents also experience more intense anger and frustration and many develop physical complaints which can last for years. Parents lose confidence and find it difficult to trust again. The whole dynamic of their family is suddenly destroyed. There is often disbelief that the loss has actually occurred. This use of denial can protect the parents for many months from experiencing the stark reality of the death. Social withdrawal is also common and this can deprive parents of the support which is offered.

Parents' pain can often be intensified by the way in which they learn of their child's death. On many occasions, breaking the bad news is left to doctors or members of the emergency services. There is an urgent need for additional training for these professionals so that they can learn how to ease the pain for parents through a sympathetic and kind approach. Kindness, in particular, is greatly appreciated by the parents at such a difficult time. Many years later, parents can distinctly remember who informed them of the death and whether or not they appeared to care.

As in SIDS death, accidental death allows no time for preparation or for anticipatory mourning on the part of parents, which might help to soften the blow. The initial intense numbness, confusion and disbelief are soon replaced by feelings of anxiety and helplessness, with feelings of emptiness and hopelessness predominating. These are often followed, shortly after, by gut-wrenching sadness, bitterness and intense anger, occasionally directed at the dead child. In parallel with these emotional reactions are the physical effects of the loss, such as loss of appetite, insomnia and a feeling of complete and utter exhaustion. An intense physical pain is frequently felt in the lower chest area which may be quite frightening for the parents and may be accompanied by palpitations of the heart. Guilt is another feature, with parents frequently blaming themselves or their partner. 'If only we had done, or not done, this or that then maybe our child might have lived!' Many parents become depressed at a later stage of this grieving process and suicidal thoughts are not uncommon.

The shock of a child's sudden death impacts negatively on all members of the family. The dead child's siblings may even feel partly responsible for the death if they had some responsibility for caring for the child at the time of death. Their need for comfort and support often goes unmet as their parents are so preoccupied with the death of the child, and because of the intensity of their grief are unable to offer sufficient support. Some studies have shown an increase in alcohol abuse and marital breakdown following the sudden death of a child. These families have an enormous need for comfort and support. This can be provided through the patience and understanding of family and friends. It must be understood that these parents can never be the same again and normality, as they knew it before, can never return. The family dynamic can be compared to a jigsaw puzzle with one piece constantly missing. They must be allowed to share their pain and relive events over a prolonged period of time if they are ever to resolve their grief. The reality of their loss cannot be changed and all they can do is learn to adapt to it.

DEATH FOLLOWING PROLONGED ILLNESS is one of the few types of death in childhood which is expected. It is obvious, therefore, that parents would have an opportunity to adjust to the impending death of their child and many go through a process known as 'anticipatory grieving'. Although this aspect may appear to be a redeeming feature, the unique strain and stress which prolonged terminal illness can place on all members of the family, and particularly on the marital relationship, cannot be overstated. The reaction to the diagnosis of a terminal illness can be quite different in both parents. Fathers frequently cope through denial and bury themselves in their work, leaving the mother unsupported. In fact, close friends can provide more support for the mother than the father in many instances, particularly when the mother is given the primary responsibility for caring for the child during the interim phase between diagnosis and death. Anticipatory grieving, which diminishes the severity of the grieving process following the death, with less evidence of guilt or self-blame, less extreme emotional reaction, less anger and a lower incidence of psychiatric illness, can be facilitated only through support of the parents. However, in my experience, it is unusual for both parents to be at the same stage in the grieving process at any one time, particularly in the early stages.

For many parents, the terminal phase will have been preceded by the horror of learning of their child's life-threatening illness. The emotional cascade through which they have to travel before they can begin to come to terms with their child's illness, will take them on a journey which begins with shock and travels through disbelief, anger, denial, anxiety and depression. If either parent is unable to draw support from a spouse, this can lead to intense feelings of resentment and anger which may permanently affect the relationship in a very negative way. If their child suffers from cancer, which nowadays carries the hope of permanent cure, then the crisis which occurs at diagnosis is repeated even more intensely if their child suffers a relapse and the hope of cure is gone. A further unique feature of death following prolonged illness is the fact that the majority of dying children know that they are dying. This is certainly true, at some level or other, for children over two years of age. The child's concept of death will obviously vary with age. Whilst it is felt that children under two years of age have no concept of death, it may well be possible that children in this age-group may be able to conceptualise death at some level or other at a time when they may not have the words to speak about it. For children between two and five years of age, death is seen in terms of separation from the comfort and support of their parents. Children in this age-group use a form of magical thinking and do not see death as a permanent event. Their understanding is that if you die, you may return again after a short time.

Children between the age of six and eleven begin to understand the permanent nature of death, and death itself may well be associated with fears of mutilation or injury. By the time the twelfth year is reached, the majority of children will have developed an 'adult' concept of what death really means but cannot contemplate the possibility of their own death. In fact, this egocentricity may well be carried through into adult life. Sigmund Freud is reported to have said to his wife 'Darling, if either one of us should die before the other, I think I'll move to Paris!'

Given that the majority of children who are dying are aware of this fact, it is essential that they be offered an opportunity of sharing their fears. Because most children tell their parents only what they think their parents can cope with, this presents obvious difficulties. These difficulties can be circumvented if all dying children are presented with an opportunity to discuss their fears and worries. In my experience, it is always best to question children as to why they asked a question or made a statement rather than to assume that what they said or what they asked is actually what they meant. For example, the question 'Am I going to die?' may well be asked with a view to being reassured that death is not imminent or else to confirm what is already known.

Parents who are prepared to clearly indicate to their dying child that they are strong enough to listen to his fears and worries, will not be left with the agony of not knowing what the child knew once death has occurred. The grieving process in these parents tends, in the main, to follow a more normal course and to be less intense and less prolonged. The maturity which many dying children display may greatly impress their parents. These children may display an understanding of life and death and a wisdom far beyond their years. I have known children as young as six or seven years of age to have made a will and others to have an input into their own funeral arrangements. These dying children seem to have an understanding of how their death will affect others in the family, and through words and actions make their peace with those around them. This may involve sharing gifts and prized possessions with brothers and sisters. I have known young children reassure other children in the family that they were not afraid to die, thereby absolving other siblings from any possible guilt-feelings.

As the dying child's illness progresses and health deteriorates, resignation to the fact that death is inevitable slowly replaces the hope for survival. As death approaches, one of the major concerns of parents is how their child will die. They require enormous support at this time and, since the advent of modern palliative care, can be reassured that every effort will be made to ensure minimal discomfort for their child. If possible, parents should be supported in their efforts to allow their child to die at home. As death approaches, the dying child becomes the sole preoccupation of the parents' thoughts. Many parents go to extraordinary lengths to ensure that each day is memorable, with the realisation that soon all they will be left with are the memories of their child. They require information as to the probable mode of death and a description of how their dying child will appear and react during the last moments of life. In addition, they will require information concerning the needs of siblings around this time. The siblings themselves, depending on their ages, should be given appropriate information concerning the mode of death.

It is not unusual for some parents who have watched their child go through sickening and unpleasant treatment, to experience enormous relief for the first few weeks following the death. If the parents have been adequately advised and supported prior to the death, then funeral arrangements will have been put in place by them. If such arrangements are not in place, then the parents may be in no fit condition to make such arrangements immediately following the death. In such circumstances, the funeral arrangements are made by a close relative and this can lead to many difficulties for the parents later on. For example, the child may not be dressed as the parents would have wished, inappropriate prayers may be said at the church, the child's favourite music may not have been played or the child may well be buried at a graveyard too far from home to allow for regular visits to the grave.

With death following a prolonged illness, the intensity of grief is less than following sudden death and the process is usually less complicated. However, much depends on how the parents were supported over the years of illness that their child endured. A close relationship with the treatment team and absolute honesty at all times will usually result in an uncomplicated grieving process. Contact with the family should be maintained for a number of years to ensure that all unanswered questions can be dealt with and any concerns addressed.

WHILST FEW PARENTS WILL wish to even contemplate the possibility that their child might die, if they are forced to address this issue they will mention road traffic accidents or drowning as possibilities. Alternatively, they might consider a peaceful death at home or in hospital following a prolonged illness, the death occurring with the child surrounded by those who love it. Death of their child by murder is something which few parents can even begin to contemplate.

From a parent's perspective, there cannot be a more devastating and painful way to lose a child than through murder. As with accidental death, the loss is a sudden one and the immediate reaction is one of complete shock. Those who have to impart such horrifying news require special training if they are not to add insult to injury through lack of sensitivity in their approach. In addition, the death is also a violent one and this can present parents with enormous problems when they begin to realise that their child may have suffered the horrifying fear that death was imminent, together with the pain of the violence inflicted upon them. These horrifying thoughts, more than any other, create enormous problems for parents when they attempt to resolve their grief. A further aspect of death by murder is that the act was deliberate and therefore perhaps preventable, thereby increasing their sense of anger and guilt at the failure of the law enforcers and of themselves to protect their child. Such feelings of guilt may appear unreasonable, given the circumstances surrounding the death of the child. However, these feelings are commonly expressed by parents who have lost a child through murder. Also to be considered is the fact that death of a child by murder is different from death by suicide, in that a murdered child had no choice. Thus, death of a child by murder, because of its suddenness, associated violence, the deliberate nature of the act and the absence of choice is a form of death which is particularly devastating.

An obsession with thoughts surrounding the death of their murdered child is extremely common in parents. They become filled with dread at the thought of their child slowly bleeding to death, in agonising pain and perhaps crying out for them. An insensitive police force may deny them essential information concerning the mode of death and whether or not death was instant or delayed. They will wish to view their child's remains. If the body is badly mutilated, then expert assistance is required to make it as presentable as possible. If this is impossible, perhaps because of a delay in finding the body, then the family should be shown the most normal parts. This assists the family to accept that their child has indeed died. The forensic pathologist's report, in all its gory detail, is revealed at the inquest hearing, further adding to the parents' pain. The obvious interest of journalists, who frequently report in a most insensitive and graphic way, and of photojournalists who try to capture private and revealing moments of grief, can add greatly to the parents' pain. Newspaper reports may even question the character of the dead child and somehow suggest that their murder was partly their own fault.

Then there is the intense anger directed at the murderer and also at the criminal justice system for failing to either apprehend him or else to find him guilty. Such anger makes it almost impossible for parents to even begin to grieve and mourn the loss of their child. If the perpetrator is apprehended, then further anguish can be experienced by parents during the trial, where every effort seems to be made to protect the rights of the accused, with little attention being paid to the rights of the victims or their families. Sitting through the trial and hearing all of the gory details continues to feed the parents' pain and anger. The accused's legal team may attempt character assassination of the victim or else will attempt to have the charge reduced from murder to manslaughter on the grounds of diminished responsibility. Even if the accused is convicted of murder and is given a life sentence, we should remember that there is no such thing any longer as a 'life' sentence, with most convicted killers qualifying for parole-review after approximately ten years. The punishment which is meted out to the murderer by the criminal justice system may well be used by the parents as a yardstick for the value of their child's life. Lenient sentencing can be the final straw for some parents. For many, they wish to have their child's death avenged and this wish can become overpowering. This creates additional problems for the family who may fear that one of their own may become a murderer also.

The strain on family life becomes unbearable. We know from one American study that in approximately seventy per cent of cases, the parents end up becoming either divorced or separated. Parents tend to have too many agendas to deal with in relation to their murdered child and are therefore unavailable to one another to offer support. As one parent put it 'We are like two radio stations, broadcasting on entirely different frequencies'!

AS WELL AS HAVING to cope with all the other issues surrounding the death of their child, parents whose child committed suicide are almost paralysed by recurring guilt and the stigma associated with this mode of death. The loss of any child or loved one impacts physically, intellectually, spiritually and emotionally. However, it is the emotional trauma which seems to predominate. Most parents experience profound guilt. That their child took its own life must be seen as their failing. They feel that they should have noticed something different and have been able to predict this event. They feel as if they have failed their child in some way or other and to have missed some perceived cries for help. They also feel rejected by their child who appeared to have preferred death to living with them. Most parents are also extremely embarrassed as a result of these feelings of guilt. Society's unease with suicidal death compounds these difficulties. The stigma of suicide can affect all members of the family. Insensitive remarks add to their pain and unease. As with death by murder, death caused by suicide is followed by an inquest. The family, once more, have to sit through the medical findings which describe in great detail the physical effects created by the mode of death. Frequently, the results of the inquest are publicised, causing further embarrassment to the family.

The quest for many parents is to attempt to understand why their child took its own life. Most of us find the act of self-destruction extremely difficult to comprehend. Parents may experience extreme anger at the selfishness of their child who, whilst apparently taking its own life, also took part of theirs. Anger directed at their dead child creates further guilt for the parents. They need to be encouraged to talk openly about their feelings and to reach out to family and friends for help. It is also important to reassure parents that suicide, rather than being an act of rejection, is much more a statement about the individual than about anybody else. They also need to be informed that suicide is not an inherited condition and that there is no greater chance of it happening to their family again. They should understand that anyone determined to take their own life will succeed, regardless of whatever attempts are made to deter them.

I WISH TO GIVE brief consideration now to the problems created by missing children. This area has received little attention over the years, perhaps because it is a relatively rare event. When any member of a family is lost, either temporarily or permanently, there is a profound effect on all within that family. The child may be lost through an unobserved accident, through abduction, or in the case of older children, through becoming missing in action during wartime. The initial reaction on the part of parents is that of fear – fear that their child is dead. In the case of abducted children, the first few days are filled with frantic efforts to find their child. This is often followed by anger, often directed at the police authorities when their efforts to find the child are perceived as being inadequate. These families suffer the same painful emotional reaction as any family who lose a child, but in these cases unresolved grief becomes the norm. Because they have no evidence that their child is dead, their loss cannot truly become a reality. They continue to hope and to pray that one day their child will be found alive and well. Because their grief is unresolved, the stress which they have to bear is both prolonged and indefinite.

For the parents of those older children who are missing in action during times of war, there is the added problem that, if their child were married at the time, it is his wife and family who receive all of the support and condolences, whilst their own needs remain unmet. These parents feel a distressing sense of powerlessness and helplessness. Many become consumed by constant thoughts of the missing child. Conversation at home centres around the missing child, with the result that brothers' and sisters' needs are often neglected. If the missing child was older and its parents, through old-age, had become dependent on him, then the loss can be even more devastating. Support for parents in this situation needs to be infinitely patient and prolonged.

FOR PARENTS, THE LOSS of a child is the most devastating loss of all. For most couples, their best support in times of distress is their spouse. Unfortunately, with the death of a child, both partners are simultaneously affected and the person to whom each would normally turn for support is struggling to survive their own grief. This loss of support from a partner is a second great loss which each parent encounters. This can produce anger in one partner, with the other compounding their pain. The most stable of marital relationships can be plunged into chaos and disarray following the death of a child. There is a much greater effect on parents whose relationship, prior to the loss of their child, is far from ideal. Further suffering is caused when one partner sees the pain which the other is having to endure.

Another difficulty for parents is that they may feel that each partner is at the same stage of the grieving process at the same time. It is important for parents to realise

71

that, whilst each of them is a parent of the same dead child, their individual loss may be quite different. This is because each parent has developed a unique relationship with the child throughout its life. For example, a mother may have spent significantly more time in contact with her child than the father. Her feelings of loss on the death of her child may be much more acute because of the absolute disruption of her normal daily routine which involved feeding, dressing, touching and listening to her child.

The father's pain may be more acute at weekends, at a time when he would normally have most contact with the child, and he might find the workplace a place of sanctuary from his pain. The mother, on the other hand, may have little respite, given that the daily house chores need to be continued, particularly if there are other surviving children. Such routines, of which the dead child was a part, may only serve to heighten her sense of loss. These differences in grieving between each parent may give rise to misinterpretation of the degree of loss which each member feels for the dead child. It is therefore essential for each parent to understand that there is no proper way to grieve and that grief for each of them will be a unique experience. While many of these difficulties will be absent when a single parent is grieving for a lost child, such a parent may be forced to make all of the decisions at a time when he or she is clearly unable to as a result of their intense pain.

The significance of the impact of the death of a child on its siblings has been underestimated. The effect on these siblings can sometimes be devastating, particularly so with decreasing family size, in that now following the death of one child, there may be only one remaining child in that family. Also, as previously mentioned, surviving siblings have to live with the loss caused by such deaths for a much longer time than their parents. The problems created by the death are dependent on the relationship which the remaining children had with the dead child and from the reaction of their parents to such a loss. In the case of death following a prolonged illness, jealousies may have developed because of the special attention which the ill child

72

was receiving and, in such circumstances, other children in the family may fantasise or wish for the death of the child. At certain ages, children imagine that they can make things happen by just wishing for them. If this is the case, then feelings of guilt become a huge problem for these children who feel that they are somehow responsible for the death.

The attitude which the parents adopt at the death of a child can have a profound influence on the surviving children. If parents idealised the dead child, then the surviving children cannot even begin to match the 'perfection' of that child. Following the death of a child, parents may become over-protective, particularly if there is only one remaining child left in that family. This over-protection can be quite stunting to the development of independence in surviving children and can result in timid children, totally lacking in confidence. Other parents may, through their behaviour, establish the ground-rule which insists that the dead child is no longer spoken of in the household. This attitude may be adopted so that further pain can be avoided through mention of the dead child. However, such an approach prevents mention of feelings of guilt and therefore resolution of grief.

If all family members are aware that for each of them their grief will be unique and if open discussion and support for one another is available, then the death of a child can have some positive effects for all. They can all incorporate the loss into their lives and this can strengthen family bonds. This is the key to survival, and this sharing will provide the courage to work through the grieving process and to be able to visualise a meaningful future, despite the loss.

Those who come into contact with families who have suffered such a tragic loss must be conscious of the depth of grief which family members are suffering. They must be aware of their capacity to add to that pain through an insensitive approach. We must not be judgmental or make assumptions which have no foundation. We should not avoid mention of the dead child in their presence for fear of adding to their pain. In my experience, parents are pleased when their child is remembered and when they see that the child has had an effect on others with whom he has come into contact. Please do not tell them that they should be happy at 'having an angel in Heaven'! All parents would prefer to have their 'little devil' with them on earth! Neither should we claim to 'know how you feel' if we have not been through a similar loss. Unless we have, then we cannot know what pain their loss is causing them. What grieving parents and siblings need is understanding, patience, sympathetic support and, more than anything else, time. With such support, the task of completing the grief work and achieving some resolution of grief can indeed be accomplished.

DEATH AND OLD AGE

DR MARGO WRIGLEY

OLD AGE IS SEEN as a time of ill-health, physical frailty and confusion. These assumptions lead to the erroneous conclusion that dying and death itself are not significant issues for old peole. This is far from the truth. Most old people, until they reach their mid-seventies, are mentally and physically healthy and they enjoy life. Most live in their own homes. It is, therefore, hardly surprising that the death of others or the experience of dying are traumatic events for older people.

Changes in life expectancy have had a profound effect on the experience of dying in old age. Most people now live until their mid- to late seventies. Two-thirds of people who die do so in institutions. What this means is that death has become a relatively unfamiliar event since it is largely confined to old age, and those who die are unlikely to do so in their own homes. These changes affect both those dying and those who are bereaved.

This chapter proposes to examine death and dying in old age from a personal and practical point of view. It will then examine death and dying in dementia – a condition which most commonly occurs in old age and has special features which make death and dying particularly poignant for relatives.

OLDER PEOPLE ARE CONSCIOUS of their own mortality and so think about their impending death. Probably as a consequence of this they are, in general, less anxious than younger people about death. As part of preparing for death older people may at times wish to discuss death with other members of their family, but the response of their family may inhibit such discussion. This is a pity because a useful function is served by such openness and is ultimately helpful to both parties. The reluctance of younger people to engage in such discussions reflects the modern denial of death which is in part related to the reduced opportunity to witness death and participate in its rituals.

An integral part of preparation for death is 'life review'. Older people often reminisce about their past life and this review serves the useful psychological function of allowing a sense of completeness to develop, a sense that life has been well-traversed. In others, this review may be tinged with sadness for lost opportunites or for acts regretted, and in these people preparation for death is difficult and may be resisted or, in some, result in depressive illness.

Death can be a protracted experience for older people if they gradually die from chronic, progressive, distressing and sometimes painful conditions. In these circumstances especially, they express fears of dying alone and of dying without dignity.

Some older people may anticipate their death with relief because it is seen by them as a means of rejoining loved ones who have died or as an escape from a chronic, painful physcial condition. In this context, it is relevant to consider the will to live. Some people seem to lose the will to live for various reasons and yet there are others who, despite all the odds, will struggle to continue with life until a particular anniversary or landmark birthday has been passed and then almost happily die.

OBVIOUSLY, ELDERY PEOPLE ARE much more likely to experience the death of a person close to them – be it friend or relative – than younger people. For instance, widowhood occurs in three-quarters of all women. This does not mean they become more resilient to bereavement. Conversely, for many, the effects of a death may be profound. Situations in which this is likely are where the death is of a spouse or of a child or if the bereaved person has been the carer of the deceased. Similarly, the experience of the death of a close relative or friend can be difficult to accept if one is in residential care. In addition, younger people no longer experience death as in the past, for instance by attending wakes, so they are less able to help and support their older relatives and friends during the time following a significant death. Finally, such a death may lead to thoughts of their own eventual death.

Grief in older people is broadly similar to grief in younger people. The same phases of numbness followed by depression and, finally, acceptance occur. The point cannot be made too strongly that the phases vary in their duration and may overlap. In some, resolution of grief occurs in six months, whilst in others two years or more is required.

During the period of grief the person frequently feels physically unwell and typically complains of fatigue. Psychological symptoms are common and include low mood, anxiety and problems with concentration and memory. In one study of elderly recently bereaved people, one-third reported visual hallucinations in the form of seeing the dead person, and one-half reported illusions in which they misinterpreted objects such as curtains as the dead person. Far from being frightened, as one would expect, most considered such experiences as helpful and comforting. In some, low mood is a serious problem and becomes a depressive illness requiring treatment in its own right. Many studies confirm that bereaved elderly people are at high risk of successful suicide, so depression should always be taken seriously and vigorously treated in this group of people. Denial has also been described as a prominent feature in this age-group with the person behaving as though nothing has happened. This response is invariably followed by problems later in adjusting to bereavement.

It is of note that psychological symptoms may be worse in those with poor physical health or who have limited physical activity. One often quoted study found an increased rate of death from cardiovascular disease in recently bereaved elderly men in the year after the death of a spouse. 'They died of a broken heart'. Many factors following such a death may be operating here, such as poor eating patterns and, therefore, impaired health.

WHO IS LIKELY TO have a traumatic response to a bereavement? If the relationship between the bereaved and the dead person was poor or complicated, grief may be prolonged or abnormal. Likewise, a sudden death is more difficult to adjust to. The circumstances of death are highly relevant. If death has been by suicide, adjustment is very hard – not just because of the violent and angry nature of the act but also because other people are reluctant to talk about it, so the usual expressions of grief and offers of emotional support are not as forthcoming.

However, certain aspects of grief are special in old age, as are certain circumstances, and these will now be mentioned. First, death of a significant figure in an older person's life may result in isolation and loneliness. Older people, in general, have a smaller circle of close friends and relatives. It is not unusual in a very old person for there to be only one other person they are close to. The death of that person is irreplaceable – not just because of the uniqueness of the person but because older people have considerably fewer opportunities for making new friends.

Death of a spouse in old age is no less painful than in earlier years. In some ways it may be worse. Other people may not be so sympathetic, commenting 'You had a good innings together', and fail to appreciate the enormity of the loss. Again, there is the permanency of the gap left with little opportunity of remarrying, especially for widows. An equally unhelpful, though well-intentioned, response of some families is to take over and run the person's life. This is particularly true for widows and may mean that independence is lost or not gained in those who have always leant heavily on their spouse. Widows may unwisely move in with children without due consideration being given to the move by either party. The widow sees it as a refuge and the child as a kindness. Such major decisions should always be left for some considerable time, perhaps for a year. Equally, recently bereaved elderly people may shift the balance of their relationships with their children and come to expect, even demand, more attention and help with practical matters. This, too, is undesirable and should be discouraged, with children promoting independence by facilitating the development of other social outlets. This response is particularly likely in women who, again, have been very dependent on their spouses and have not acquired essential everyday living skills such as dealing with bank accounts. Likewise, men with few domestic skills may become dependent on their children rather than acquire such skills after the death of their partner. There is an important preventative message here – we should all ensure that we are capable of managing our day to day affairs.

The death of an elderly person's child is especially difficult to accept – usually it is the result of an accident or malignant illness. The feelings such a death causes are complex. The grief is enormous – often coloured with guilt. 'Why am I still alive' is often said by the bereaved parent and tremendous anger can ensue. Depressive illness is not unusual, often with suicidal ideas and sometimes bizarre behaviour – the only way the person has of expressing their grief. The death of an adult child can be every bit as traumatic as that of a small child for an elderly parent.

If an elderly person is in institutional care when a significant death occurs, they may not be involved in funeral arrangements and as a consequence become very distressed. Where possible, such people should attend funerals and be given the chance to mourn properly. Equally, the death of a fellow-resident can be distressing. Sometimes a friend is lost through the death but, in all cases, it foreshadows the person's own death and how it is likely to be dealt with in the institution.

AT THE TIME OF death, practical assistance for instance with funeral arrangements, together with opportunities to meet others and talk about the death, thereby assimilating it, are enormously helpful as is the opportunity to talk about the bereavement after the acute phase. Continued social support from family and friends after a bereavement is of immense help. This includes practical help and emotional support, but it should not overwhelm the bereaved older person to such an extent that they are at risk of losing their independence –

a particular vulnerability in older people.

The consequences of death influence the adjustment to bereavement. Paradoxically, it has been found that consequences can be both positive and negative. Elderly widows may describe feelings of depression and anxiety but at other times feel a sense of improved self-esteem and mastery because they have assumed a decision-making role and they have taken on responsibilities for matters normally dealt with by their husbands. The ability of the older person to carry out the tasks of daily living, such as cooking, is important in how they adjust to bereavement. Those who are most competent have fewer problems.

THOSE WHO ARE LIKELY to have a traumatic response to grief have been mentioned already. In this context, the bereaved person's coping strategies are an important component determining, in part, the response to a bereavement. Those who are inclined to avoid or ignore their grief, or who blame themselves for the death of their loved ones, may run into difficulties later. This adverse response may be the person's usual response to problems, but it may also be the psychological mechanism the person subconsciously uses to deal with a traumatic bereavement. The trauma may be inherent in the relationship between the bereaved and the dead person or it may be a consequence of the circumstances in which the person died, for instance an unexpected or violent death.

Abnormal responses to grief are diverse and include denial and the development of anxiety or depression. Occasionally, bizarre behaviour or somewhat histrionic behaviour may ensue as the manifestation of the person's grief. In a similar vein, others appear confused especially if very elderly. Sometimes, the death of a spouse can uncover dementia in the surviving partner – the latter's disabilities becoming exposed by their abler partner's death. Occasionally, a bereaved person turns to alcohol to obliterate grief.

MANY THINGS MAY HELP with abnormal grief, but what is needed varies from situation to situation. Grief counselling is quite widely available now. Special approaches in old age include 'reminiscence' in which a life-review is formally carried out, thereby allowing the person to regain some sense of their own identity and also internalise or incorporate the dead person within their memories, thus aiding resolution of grief.

Support groups can be very helpful if people are isolated as a consequence of their bereavement. Experiences are shared with others in a similar situation, coping strategies exchanged and, sometimes, friends made.

In some cases, help with acquiring skills to deal with either business or domestic issues must be learnt, and for a few, formal help is required.

Medical assistance is necessary if depression is suspected. The bereaved person should be encouraged to attend their family doctor who may, in certain cases, particularly if suicide is a risk, refer the person to a psychiatrist. Likewise, the family doctor may be able to assist if alcohol abuse is occurring. In the case of an uncovered dementia, assessment followed by the involvement of other members of the family and appropriate support services, can be initiated via the person's family doctor. It is important that if an abnormal grief response is suspected help is sought.

Finally, it cannot be stressed enough that moving house shortly after the bereavement should be discouraged. The potential loss of identity should be highlighted to the bereaved person, as well as the loss of closeness with the deceased spouse if such a move is undertaken.

DEMENTIA IS A CONDITION characterised by gradual loss of a person's intellectual ability, their ability to care for themselves and a change in their personality towards one of profound apathy and marked social withdrawal. Apart from the earlier stages of dementia, consideration of the perspective of relatives with regard to death and dying is of greater importance than the perspective of the sufferer. Relatives sometimes liken the process of dementia to one of seeing a loved one die in front of their eyes whilst they are still alive in a body. Coupled with this is an ever-increasing dependence on relatives which may lead to frustration, anger and guilt in conjunction with the role of caring, and equally, frustration and anger at the waste of the person so afflicted. The interaction between these diverse emotions results in complicated grief reactions. It is sometimes said that because the person, as it were, psychologically and intellectually dies before physical death occurs, that grieving takes place prior to the actual death. The question, therefore, arises as to whether grief is reduced afterwards. It may not be. These and other issues will now be examined.

IN THE EARLY STAGES of dementia insight may be retained, by which is meant that the person realises his/her memory is failing, or less precisely is aware that something is wrong at a certain level and is distressed as a consequence. In some, this distress takes the form of a grief reaction. It is helpful to allow the person to talk about their feelings whilst accepting this will be limited by the person's impaired memory. Others may develop depression which requires treatment, generally with anti-depressants. Later, assisting the person to take practical measures to minimise their disabilities is useful. In all cases, emotional support and encouragement is essential to improve the person's self-confidence, enabling them to feel liked and valued despite their disabilities. Later, insight is lost because the dementing process itself reduces the ability to conceptualise the disabilities which are an integral part of dementia, and with this comes relief from the symptoms of grief.

One area frequently not appreciated is the grief felt, albeit in a confused fashion, by some dementia sufferers if a spouse or someone close to them dies. It is not unusual for such a person to be totally excluded from funeral arrangements and the consequence of this can be catastrophic. Disturbed behaviour, with agitation and aggression as an expression of the loss may occur, as can depression. It is therefore important, where possible, to include the person in funeral arrangements and be prepared to go over events many times in a gentle way until assimilation of the death has occurred at some level.

DEMENTIA POSES VERY SPECIAL issues for relatives partly because it is a chronic progressive process lasting many years. Also there are three features of the condition which have a particular bearing on the reaction of the carer who is often an equally elderly spouse.

First, dementia in the spouse, with its attendant personality changes, means that for many there is a loss of that person in life. Carers frequently use euphemisms such as describing the person as being an empty shell.

Secondly, hand in hand with the change in personality comes an increasing loss of self-care skills and consequent increasing dependence on relatives. In the later stages of dementia it means that the person requires twenty-four hour care and poses a substantial burden for relatives. However, the burden of care is not only physical but also psychological because there is little return for carers in that the sufferer, no longer recognising their relatives, may react in an aggressive fashion towards them, perceiving them to be intrusive strangers.

The third factor which can complicate grief in the relatives of dementia sufferers is the behavioural changes which are an integral part of the condition. These can include wrongful accusations towards relatives, such as accusing them of stealing possessions, starving them and failing to visit. Failure to recognise relatives is common, as indeed is referring to them as parents, and this emphasises the role-reversal which occurs for adult children. Furthermore, it is difficult to continue caring for someone who does not recognise you. Aggressive behaviour of either a verbal or physical nature can be a major problem in some sufferers, and not only physically inhibits care being provided but also psychologically inhibits such care. Occasionally, in dementia sufferers, disinhibited sexual behaviour may occur, and again this can have a deleterious psychological effect on carers. Other behavioural changes which add to the burden of care are wandering, sleep disturbance, loss of interest and communication problems.

These three features, superimposed on the phases of mourning, often lead to complicated grief reactions in the relatives of dementia sufferers. Into this complicated picture must be set the phases of mourning which follow the same sequence, albeit of different form and duration, as the mourning which follows on death itself.

The initial stage of numbness is caused by disbelief at the onset of symptoms – the disbelief may be worse if accompanied by profound changes in the sufferer's personality. Further numbness may follow on being told of the diagnosis. Time and understanding help relatives through this phase. However, some relatives may attempt to cope by denial – in other words, there is a refusal to accept the diagnosis. This leads to unrealistic hopes of a cure, occasionally to poor and inadequate care which, in some instances, may leave the sufferer at risk if proper safeguards are not put in place for the person. Again, time and understanding supplemented by information is the best approach. Subsequently, distress emerges – the depth of which is related to the quality of the relationship between the relative and sufferer prior to diagnosis and also to how long the process has been going on. All sorts of emotions can occur such as sadness, anger and anxiety – sadness at the losses caused by the dementia, anger felt and sometimes expressed in all directions, and finally very real anxiety if the dementia is of the inherited variety such as Huntington's chorea. Again, patience and time to listen are important for relatives. At a certain stage, relatives move to a phase of coping where practical help is of the essence. Even then, emotional support is essential whether it is from other relatives, friends or professionals.

Moving to institutional care is also a stage of bereavement and relatives may find it difficult to come to terms with such a move. There may be a sense of failure or regret that they were unable to continue caring. Often carers say 'I promised I would care until the end', and feel bitterly disappointed that they have been unable to do so.

MOST PEOPLE CONSIDER THAT once the dementia sufferer has died, relatives feel an enormous lifting of the burden and sense of relief at the death. Experience indicates that, for many relatives, this is not the case. This is particularly so if they have been burdened by excessive care demands prior to the person's death. They may be unduly condemnatory of the care they have provided and feel guilty, concluding that they did not do enough for the person. In addition, paradoxically, they may miss the person and miss their role as carer. Caring for a dementia sufferer is such a heavy burden that often there is a narrowing of the person's life to such an extent to accommodate the demands of the dementia sufferer, that a void exists after death.

Other relatives may feel enormous relief when the death of the sufferer eventually occurs. They may feel guilty about this but should be reassured that this is quite normal. However, it is worth noting that one study found that even in people who react to the death of their relative with relief, the emergence of depression was not uncommon one year later.

Anticipatory grief refers to experiencing a loss before it has actually occurred – for example, imagining the death of a person whilst he/she is in the midst of a terminal illness such as dementia. The question arises as to whether it is of value where relatives of dementia sufferers are concerned. The general experience of providing care to a loved one is distressing and physically taxing for older adults. One study found that the death of the dementia sufferer did not reduce the psychological distress experienced afterwards, which in part dispels the notion that anticipatory grief is useful. Easing the physical burden of care may be helpful in these situations because it provides time for the carer to come to terms with the situation. However, in dementia there is a series of changes in the person's condition which can cause distress to relatives, resulting in a re-emergence of grief. Information about the stages of dementia and what one might expect at each stage may ease the distress and help adjustment to the situation.

IT IS NOW BECOMING clearer that attention to carers and relatives is crucial both before and at the time of death. The sort of help that carers and relatives require varies greatly, depending upon their situation, coping strategies and their personalities.

Information about the condition is considered important. Relatives should know what to expect, what to do about particular problems, what help is available and how it may be obtained.

Emotional support is of great assistance to many relatives. This can be provided by both family and friends and also by professionals.

Special voluntary organisations such as the Alzheimer Society of Ireland have a particular role in providing information and they also run support groups which are very helpful to many people. But again, it should be kept in mind that individuals vary. Not everyone feels a support group is helpful to them but may prefer to take the attitude of 'one day at a time' rather than anticipating what may lie ahead of them.

Practical help is essential to reduce the burden of care. This has the added benefit of providing the carer with time to start the grieving process. Easing the physical burden of care can obviously be done by other family members and also by professional services such as home-helps and meals-on-wheels.

There is an assumption that the carer's problems are over once the dementia sufferer has died – but this is far from the case. As described earlier, feelings following the person's death are very complicated and this reinforces the need for continuing support at this time. For this reason the funeral, as a public expression of the person's death, is pivotal in facilitating grieving. It also allows the bereaved to reflect on the person as he/she originally was. During this time it is important to acknowledge the work of the carer and to provide opportunities for discussion whilst the carer tries to rebuild his/her life. The grief following the death of a dementia sufferer is even more poignant than usual because of the loss of years of life – for the carer as well as the sufferer. This is even more painful when the sufferer is a young person and where perhaps children have lost a parent not just by death but prior to that, through the process of dementia itself.

ABNORMAL GRIEF

DR ANTHONY O'FLAHERTY

IT IS SAID THAT it is better to have loved and lost then never to have loved at all. The price of love and detachment is grief. We grieve when we lose the object of our attachment. This response – grief – is the most appropriate response to loss and if it is completed and resolved has the virtue of being a healing response. If we do not grieve we will suffer psychologically and physically.

There are two phases in grief:

1) Recognition and psychological acceptance.
2) Psychological healing, which restores the person's emotional equilibrium and allows him or her to resume 'normal' living.

In understanding abnormal grief and its many facets, we must understand what normal grieving is about so that we may compare and contrast it with the abnormal.

A common question asked is 'How long do we grieve for?' There is no simple answer. Even in a situation which is quite uncomplicated, the grieving process may take from eighteen months to two years. When the death is more traumatic, then the grieving process will take much longer. It is important to remember that there is no specific time for grieving; people do it in their own time and in their own way.

Many writers talk about stages, or phases, of grief as if we go blithely from one stage or phase to another. We do not. Some days we may be coping brilliantly, while on other days we may feel hopeless and spend the day in bed. If we are to look for phases, we may say there are three:

1) *Stage of numbness.*
2) *Stage of suffering.* Here we experience pain – both physical and psychological. We experience anxiety, pangs of depression, pining, searching, guilt feelings, anger, illusions, insomnia and increased dreaming.
3) *Recovery.* Here our pain becomes less. We think less negative thoughts. We become interested in ourselves again and we can talk about the deceased without experiencing great pain and sadness.

THERE ARE MANY TYPES of abnormal grieving patterns, but the majority have a common core. This is the process of numbing or denial. When we first experience a loss, our lives are thrown into turmoil and our immediate reaction is one of disbelief. The pain of previous loss may be reactivated and we may feel frightened for our own lives.

In order to cope with this pain and chaos, we may unconsciously call up our defences so that we may fend off such unpleasant experiences. These defences allow us to function in the short-term by allowing us to be numbed from the reality that has taken place. This numbness, or denial, is useful in the short-term in that it allows us to cope with the aftermath of the death, such as the funeral, the taking care of visitors and the funeral arrangements.

In the long-term, denial or numbness is dangerous because it prevents us from recognising that loss has taken place and, therefore, prevents us from entering the second stage of grieving, namely the healing process.

A good rule of thumb is: 'the longer the numbing, the worse the reaction will be when it arrives.' Our aim then should be to shorten the period of numbing by whatever means possible. This involves encouraging people to view the deceased, to go to the funeral and to see the loss as it really is. Many people will try and avoid viewing a deceased person as they fear that this image will be the image that will remain with them. This is not so. It will be replaced by a previous and more pleasant image after a time.

We should also try to avoid creating an artificial numbness by taking tranquillisers, sleeping tablets and alcohol.

Tranquillisers and sleeping tablets, if they are to be used, should be used only when there is great distress and for as short a period as possible.

THE FOLLOWING ARE SOME specific types of abnormal grief reactions:

1) *Chronic grief.* Here the person never comes to terms with their loved one's death and they continue to grieve for the rest of their lives. It is an unpleasant condition and as time goes on, there is less and less sympathy and understanding from friends and relations.

Chronic grief usually occurs when the loss is overwhelming. It often occurs in women who are overly-dependent on their husbands and who have little or no interests or friendships outside their marriage. It also occurs in close mother-daughter relationships or after a traumatic or violent death.

For those in a state of chronic grieving, they are continually tearful, have symptoms of anxiety, are pining and are often consumed by excess guilt and anger. This anger may further alienate them from the wider community – a community which already may be alienated by the endless grief of the bereaved.

The chronic griever will also idealise the loved one whom they have lost, and whereas idealisation is a normal part of grieving and is usually short-lived, in a chronic griever it is long-term. Other features include speaking of the deceased in the present tense, dreaming of the deceased as if he or she were still alive and an inability to make other relationships.

An example of chronic grief from history is Queen Victoria. It is said that she had her husband's clothes laid out each morning and evening as if he were still alive. And her anger at her son, whom she blamed for her husband's death, prevented her from allowing him to succeed to the throne. Many of us know people in our own community who are in a state of chronic grief. They need our help and understanding. From a treatment point of view, they are quite resistive to therapy.

2) Inhibited or delayed grief. Here a large part or all of the grieving process is postponed and may be reactivated many months or years later. The predominant feature here is denial and the survivor may appear outwardly to be functioning normally. They may prosper in their jobs and may appear emotionally intact. But they will rarely, if ever, talk about the deceased and they will never show any signs of normal grieving.

Postponed grief may again occur where the loss has been too great to accept, but it may also occur when the loss is complicated by feelings of hate for the deceased. This ambivalence – love and hate – will be repressed.

THERE ARE MANY FACTORS in our personalities which affect the outcome in bereavement. If many of these occur in one person, then the likelihood of inhibited or delayed grief is greater. These factors include:

a) Losses and separations during childhood: We know that people who have experienced losses and separations during their early years are more vulnerable and cope less well with bereavement.

b) Losses in later life: We know that losses accumulate and if we are still grieving for one loss when another occurs, we may function by totally repressing the second.

c) A previous depressive illness may, out of fear, force us to avoid grieving in order to avoid a return to a depressive state.

d) It is well known that other life crises prior to or following bereavement may make grieving impossible. These include separation or divorce, retirement, children leaving home or moving house. The bereaved may focus on one of these traumas to the exclusion of their grieving.

e) Death by suicide or sudden or violent death, particularly where the body is missing, may make grieving particularly difficult. The absence of the body, the lack of ritual and the lack of a resting place deprive the bereaved of their mourning.

f) The death of a young person may be impossible to comprehend and may lead to inhibited grief. Here we should mention the huge rise in suicide among teenagers. In the United States of America, suicide is the third leading cause of death among young people in the age-group of fifteen to twenty-four years. The deaths of these young people leave shattered and bewildered families whose grief is often repressed. But when it does occur, it is compounded by guilt, anger and the need to understand. Other factors which may inhibit our grief include poverty, which may be so overwhelming that our grief must take a back-seat. Physical illness may be severe and interfere with normal grieving.

Perhaps one of the most common contributors to delayed grief, particularly in men, is a belief that to show emotions is to be weak. Some countries and cultures encourage this notion – the 'stiff upper lip' attitude. Many men who lose their wives feel that they must be 'strong' for the sake of the children. Being 'strong' means repressing their feelings, often throwing themselves into excess activity and spending longer hours at work. They fear being alone and they discourage others from expressing their feelings. They need to be made aware that you cannot get through grief unless you experience it. If you deny it, it will be prolonged.

Delayed or inhibited grief may last for months or years and can often be triggered by an emotional experience, such as a wedding, a funeral or a religious experience. The repressed grief then breaks through and can be very severe. We have seen many people whose grief has been delayed for ten or more years. One can imagine how difficult it is for the bereaved and those around them to come to terms with such emotional turmoil when such a long interval has passed between the loss and the grieving.

THE COMMONEST AFFECTIVE DISORDERS are depression and elation. Elation is an uncommon sequel to bereavement and, because of its symptoms, is also unusual. Elation is signified by an abnormally and persistently elevated, expansive or irritable mood. Persons with elation may show inflated self-esteem, grandiosity and a decreased need for sleep. They may be more talkative than usual, have flights of ideas and may be easily distracted. There may also be an increase in goal-directed activity, either socially, at work or sexually. The person may overspend, be sexually indiscreet or make foolish decisions during this time. Obviously if the above features occur with any severity, it will be noticed quite quickly and appropriate referral initiated.

The normal depression in those who are bereaved is described as 'pangs of depression'. These are feelings of intense pain and loneliness and are often experienced as a physical pain in the chest. They are at their most frequent and are most severe between the fifth and fourteenth days following bereavement when they occur without warning, at any place and at any time. Later in the grieving process, they occur on special occasions, such as birthdays or anniversaries, when one is reminded of the deceased, or at Christmas and Easter. We often call this an 'anniversary reaction' and it is quite normal.

An alternative type of depression may occur which is not normal. This may occur in those who have suffered from depression in the past or may occur in those who have never suffered from depression before. In the latter group, it can be missed and can be mistaken for the normal grieving process. This type of depression we call 'major' or 'clinical' depression and it can vary from mild to severe depending on the severity of its symptomatology. Its features are as follows:

Depressed mood which is present for most of the day, every day, and is not reactive to environmental factors.
The depression is usually worse in the morning and improves slightly as the day progresses.
The person may awaken early and spend the early hours dreading the day.
There will be markedly decreased interest in almost all

activities, including work, home and family, with loss of libido.

Other features include loss of appetite with weight loss, insomnia with early morning waking and fatigue, feelings of guilt and worthlessness, low self-esteem, poor concentration and memory, a preoccupation with death and recurring thoughts of death. Suicidal thoughts are further unpleasant symptoms.

It is vitally important that we recognise such depression, because active and immediate treatment is indicated and is effective. Following resolution of the depression, the grieving process may progress in the normal way.

Many people suffer from physical disorders following bereavement. Surveys show us that bereaved women visit their doctors much more frequently in the year following bereavement than before. Their symptoms are real and are thought in psychological terms to be a displacement of their psychological pain by a physical one. It may also be that following bereavement our resistance is low and we are, therefore, much more prone to infections.

ANXIETY AND FEAR ARE part of the normal grieving process. They are uncomfortable to experience, are most intense soon after the loss and they gradually fade away. In a small minority of bereaved, anxiety symptoms persist to an abnormal degree. The commonest physical features of anxiety are as follows: rapid heartbeat with palpitations, loss of appetite, inability to relax, dry mouth, sweating palms, constriction in the throat, nausea, abdominal cramps with more frequent bowel motions, dizziness, tinnitus, headache, yawning and swallowing. These are accompanied by psychological symptoms, such as apprehension, feelings of insecurity and self-blame, poor concentration, poor recent memory, irritability, a fear of disease and dying, insomnia and nightmares.

The bereaved may not have all of these features together, but I am sure you will agree that even a few can be most unpleasant.

Abnormal anxiety and fear is most common following

sudden violent deaths, such as sudden infant death syndrome, suicide or homicide.

When we experience great fear and anxiety, we feel as if we have no control over our minds and our bodies. Our resultant feelings of insecurity may force us to remain at home in order to avoid the embarrassment of losing control. This becomes a vicious circle as we become even more isolated and become ever more insecure and fearful.

In extreme cases, anxiety and fear produce panic attacks. These are described as discrete periods of intense fear and discomfort. They usually occur 'out of the blue'. They are not the result of exposure to a situation that always caused anxiety in the past and they are not triggered by situations in which the person was the focus of others' attention. Common features are as follows: a shortness of breath or smothering sensation, dizziness or faintness, palpitations, trembling, sweating, choking, nausea, a desire to urinate or defecate, feelings of unreality, tingling sensations, hot flushes or chills, chest pain, a fear of dying, a fear of 'going mad' or going out of control. These attacks may be short-lived, but they are always followed by a period of exhaustion and a fear that they may recur.

The treatment of abnormal anxiety and panic attacks needs to be comprehensive and is best carried out by a health professional. It may include the following: a change in lifestyle, a reduction in the use of caffeine and nicotine, relaxation therapy, behaviour therapy, a change of diet, a brief use of medication, counselling and efficient sleep.

MANY BEREAVED PEOPLE SEEK relief through artificial means. Men often choose alcohol as it is easily available and, initially, its use will not cause undue concern. Alcohol, as we know, is a powerful drug and is most effective in blocking the pain of grief. It is used, therefore, for short-term gain and as a means of blocking out reality. It is, in fact, inducing artificial numbing. Where the bereaved cannot face the reality of the loss, his drinking can increase in an effort to block out reality completely. This results in the person becoming alcohol-dependent.

The signs of alcohol dependence are as follows: memory blackouts following drinking bouts, frequent intoxication or withdrawal symptoms when the person is expected to fulfil a major role or obligation at work or at home, inability to go to work on Mondays because of hangover, gulping drinks, impaired control, an inability to stop once the first drink has been taken, early-morning drinking, aggressiveness, re-morse, anxiety and neglect of self and others.

When dependence is recognised and suitable interven-tion has taken place, then the bereaved will have to com-mence grieving as if they had just suffered their loss. So in-stead of obliterating our grief, we are merely postponing it for another day.

Another method of artificially blocking out the reality of our loss is to take large quantities of tranquillisers. These are not as readily available as heretofore, but they may still look attractive to those in great psychological pain. Dependence on tranquillisers is a serious problem in itself and is signified by psychological dependence, physical withdrawal when they are discontinued, and a need to take increasing dosage to obtain the same effect. They may initially be given to the bereaved by a kindly neighbour or friend or by one's physi-cian and, thereafter, looked for on a regular basis.

When they are eventually withdrawn, and this must be done with great care, the person may suffer withdrawal symptoms, such as restlessness, poor concentration, tremor, anxiety, palpitations, hypersensitivity and many other symp-toms of anxiety. Later, the grieving process may surface and may be severe because of the time-lapse.

I mentioned earlier the fact that many bereaved people suffer from physical illness following the death of a loved one. In the past, grief was often listed as a cause of death. Some people would now scoff at such a notion, but we should not. It is not uncommon for a partner to die shortly after the death of their loved one. This is considered to be a type of 'giving up' and a losing of the will to live.

On a wider scale, it is well-recognised that there is an association between psychological problems and physical ill-ness. Following bereavement, we may develop joint pains, irritable bowel, spastic colon, high blood-pressure and many other physical illnesses. We do not know the exact mechanism by which psychological pain and loss produce or exacerbate physical disease, but we should be aware of the association. Only a thorough history taken by the General Practitioner may elicit the information required.

IN THIS CHAPTER WE have talked about abnormal grieving reactions and the problems which they cause. In order to avoid or minimise such reactions, we should try to do all in our power to promote understanding of the normal grief reaction.

We cannot prevent bereavement, but an important preventive measure is to accept the inevitability of death and to prepare for it as we might prepare for any of life's other major traumas. As many people now die in hospital, it should be possible for health professionals to help relatives accept that the patient is terminally-ill and to help patients and their relatives in the last days. This will involve openness with the patient regarding the diagnosis, judicious use of sedation and pain-relief, and privacy for the patient and the family. The majority of the population would wish to know that they were dying, yet many are not told for reasons that seem less than adequate. As a result, the last days or months of their lives may be filled with distrust, anger and resentment. The ideal is that the dying and their loved ones should anticipate and prepare for death together. This makes it easier to die with dignity and makes the grieving process somewhat easier.

It is vitally important for relatives to be present at the time of death, if they so wish. I often see people who felt cheated by hospital staff because they were not allowed to be present at the last moments. I never see people who complain about being present at this time.

Following the death, we should encourage viewing of the body, expression of sadness, attendance at the funeral service and at the funeral itself and burial. In western cultures it is now becoming unfashionable to do such things. We are encouraged to have our loved ones laid out in 'slumber rooms' where there is little encouragement for grief and mourning. We should encourage the old-fashioned wake where expressions of sorrow, remorse and open grieving were encouraged and the community paid tribute to the deceased.

We should encourage visits to the grave, and if there is no grave we should encourage the erection of a monument or a memorial to the deceased.

In summary, in order to avoid abnormal reactions we should see mourning as something essential and we should be less fearful of our grief and that of others. We should know that we have the capacity to experience and survive grief. Freud, in his famous article entitled 'Mourning and Melancholia', stated the following:

Although grief involves grave departures from the normal attitude to life, it never occurs to us to regard it as a morbid condition and hand the mourner over to medical treatment. We rest assured that after a lapse of time, it will be overcome and we look at any interference with it as inadvisable or even harmful.

If, for some reason, we go into a state of abnormal grieving, be it chronic or delayed, we may need specialised help. The most appropriate help is bereavement counselling which can be tailored to individuals or groups or both. This type of counselling is now readily available and produces positive results. There are also many self-help groups which were formed to aid people suffering as a result of specific traumas, such as cot death, perinatal death or stillbirth. These groups are both supportive and therapeutic.

DEATH BY SUICIDE

DR MICHAEL J. KELLEHER

DEATH IS LIFE'S SINGLE certainty. Most young people do not think about it or, perhaps more correctly, put such thoughts out of their minds because life for them is about living and not about dying. In the child's normal development, he differentiates himself from his social environment which is usually his parental world. The idea that he is a separate being within this world presupposes the idea that the parental social world existed before he attained his separate existence. Thus, every child is aware early in his life that personal existence is finite, because time was when he did not exist.

Most people cannot face this existential dilemma. The common defence, sanctioned by tradition, is the assumption that life is forever. For many to consider otherwise is a recipe for anxiety and depression. Those who are misfortunate enough to have their childhood worlds fractured through the death of parental figures find it psychologically more difficult to resort to this existential defence of the denial of death. For this reason, many studies have shown that those who are bereaved in childhood remain prey to mood disorder later in life.

FOR MOST OF US, death comes easily and slowly. There are many premonitory losses before the final cessation of life. Each loss or diminution of function symbolises Thanatos, who was the Greek personification of death, as opposed to Eros, who epitomises life and love. The challenge for each of us is how to accommodate to reversal without surrendering to circumstance.

For many young and early middle-aged adults, future horizons are expanding, apparently limitlessly. Middle-age for most, however, engenders an appreciation of the margins of individual existence. The perspective of youth is existentially divergent whereas from middle-age on, the future, psychologically, converges on a point of non-existence.

For most reflective people, their life history has a pattern of which they are an integral part. A full life is one where people have the opportunity to paint the whole portrait of their life's existence. Most, if not all, mature and psychologically healthy people would like to see their life unfold in all its important phases until the odyssey is complete. Frequently, however, this is not possible, usually because of illness, sometimes because of accident and, more rarely, because of suicide.

We emerge from the social and personal worlds of our parents. Their 'weltanschauung', or 'world view', becomes our first perspective in life. A few accept this view in total while others endeavour to reject it and make a break with the past. The majority, however, incorporate parental beliefs and attitudes, gradually modifying them in the light of personal experience. Parental models are important to our psychological well-being and those denied them suffer in many dimensions of life.

NO ONE KNOWS WHAT the final thoughts of the suicidal victim are. Before the matter was as thoroughly researched as it is today, researchers were more confident that they could get inside the mind of the deceased in order to better understand their actions. This was founded in the belief that all those who took their lives were distressed beyond endurance in the minutes or hours before their death. Their consciousness was said to constrict and their minds to have become overwhelmed with the burden of pain as well as the intolerability of circumstance. Death appeared to them to be the only way out of suffering. This was also the defence recently used by a British doctor who stood accused of assisting in the requested death of a patient by the giving of a lethal injection. The court, however, took the view that professionally assisted suicide was an unacceptable method for relief of pain and suffering. The Medical Council would only agree to his reinstatement on the Medical Register after he had undergone training in pain relief.

There are other less common reasons given, or surmised, for suicide. Distress and anger at one's self may be projected onto others. Two such events have imprinted themselves upon the mind of the author. In one, a young man who was rejected by his girlfriend, hanged himself outside her home which was also the business premises of her family. In another, a fourteen year-old schoolboy, attending a highly competitive British public school, hanged himself in his mother's wardrobe, having closed the door. When seen several years later, as part of a research project, the mother had not recovered from the loss and the shock of finding him dead in her bedroom.

Some cultures and groups within society legitimise suicide under particular circumstances, especially when the act is considered noble and worthy of commendation. Death by starvation for political purposes has a hallowed tradition in Ireland, at least during this century. Many would see it as offensive to describe the death of Terence MacSwiney or of Bobby Sands as suicide. The fact that their primary aim was political and that their lives were characterised by selflessness and courage does not change the fact that they were instrumental in bringing about their own deaths. In ancient times, as well, voluntary death by starvation was seen as a mark of personal nobility, particularly among the Roman Stoics.

Economic factors underlay the pressure in some societies towards suicide. The Hindu custom of suttee, which is now illegal in India, favoured the widow burning herself on her husband's funeral pyre. The Eskimos, when food was short, encouraged the elderly to remain behind to die when the group moved camp. The modern equivalent is the man who refuses expensive treatment in order to protect the family's resources. Societies also encourage, at particular times, suicide (or almost certain death) in association with aggression against a perceived enemy. The kamikaze pilot has created an indelible mark on the human imagination. The Japanese, however, have simply given a name to a common practice in wartime. Those who were encouraged to leave their trenches in the First World War faced an almost certain death, as did those who stormed the bridge in 'The Ballad of Athlone'. Many of those who defended the skies in The Battle of Britain had a nonchalant attitude to life and death. Some may have been suicidal or at least not caring if death was the outcome.

Such ambivalence to the consequences of personal actions is not confined to wartime. Many of those who engage in highly dangerous recreations have an attitude of pitting themselves against death and jousting with danger. The thrill of achievement is heightened by the possibility that death could have been the outcome, as it undoubtedly was for many others in similar sports in the past, and may well be so for the particular individual in the future. All of this may appear at variance with the stereotype of the contorted mind seeking release through voluntary death. However, in our choice of death, our motives are invariably mixed as they are in every other aspect of life.

Most people who seek to come to terms with the suicide death of a relative strive to understand what went on in his private mental world. The issue is complex, however, although some individuals may have a predominant final motive which the bereaved seek to comprehend.

THE MAJORITY OF SUICIDES are mentally ill. One study done in Britain almost thirty years ago showed that about two-thirds were depressed and another twenty per cent had a problem with alcohol. Most had been in touch with the professional services in the month before their death. The situation may not be the same now.

A study nearing completion in Cork indicates that a substantial minority is not in contact with the health services. The implication is that some may not be mentally ill and others, who are mentally ill, may not be receiving appropriate treatment. It would be wrong to assume that treatment guarantees suicide prevention. Nevertheless, it is a special tragedy if a person with a treatable illness ends his life without giving treatment a chance.

Suicide is more common with some lifestyles than with

others. Alcoholism and drug addiction have a high association with suicide. In each, temporary nirvana is sought from life's travails through the ingestion of psychoactive substances. Total or permanent oblivion is but one final step. Drugs and alcohol may have altered irrevocably the person's social status. Their situation may be genuinely parlous by the time death intervenes. Yet the road they took had many turnings before control was lost to chemical dependence. Other psychological states also have an association with suicide. These include personality disorder, schizophrenia and early dementia.

Physical suffering, in particular chronic pain and loss of bodily function, are important. Cancer, as well as fear as to the future course of the illness, may play a part. Firm, honest reassurance and explanation can be restorative. The concept of death must be broken down into its constituent parts. There is the process of dying which can, either at home or within the hospice movement, be controlled. There is the parting from relatives and life which is a natural process, well handled by those nurses and doctors who have been trained and self-selected to do so. Finally, there is death itself which is no problem to the deceased but may create a problem for the remaining relatives.

As well as psychological and physical factors, there are social determinants of suicide. Severe reversals in overvalued life-situations may be of great importance. There have been several well-publicised suicides of young people in Britain and Ireland who failed to get their desired points in state examinations. These are special tragedies, not only for the individuals but also for their families, classmates and school authorities. These occurrences, although well-publicised through the media, may be comparatively rare. Unfortunately, when given great notoriety, they may provide a model for other vulnerable young people to imitate. The situation is complicated further by the knowledge that many of those who achieve high points and get into cherished professions do not find happiness but, rather, the reverse. The points may have determined entry but suitability of personality determines satisfaction.

Many other social events can precipitate the drive towards suicide, although it is important to remember that there are no universal social or biological processes that invariably, or even frequently, result in suicide. Change of job, loss of job and threat of redundancy are important for some. Failure in marriage or a broken relationship is important in others. Excessive work, apparent loss of control over personal life circumstances, and feelings of shame at real or perceived wrongdoing may induce suicide. Nevertheless, if all the circumstances and facts of an individual's life were known to a third party, it still would not be possible to predict with certainty the event of suicide. The elements of randomness and personal choice and idiosyncrasy are ultimately beyond the mind of any other human being.

Many suicides have written detailed letters outlining the reasons why they are ending their lives. These, invariably, are incomplete in the sense that another person, in similar circumstances, would find insufficient reason to follow suit. This may be because, as in other important areas of personal life, determinants of choice are largely irrational. Most people accept that 'love is blind' even though many may endeavour to give reasons to themselves and others for their choice. This is also true in the case of suicide. Both the investigator and the perpetrator may seek reasons, in the logical sense, where only emotion and impulse exist.

AS THE CHILD'S MIRROR of life may be shattered by the death of a significant person in their environment, so also sudden death of relatives or friends may adversely affect both adults and children. Sudden deaths are more difficult to cope with than gradual death through illness. There are further special difficulties when the deceased is at the threshold of adult life or where life's portrait, as described earlier, is incompletely drawn. The sense of waste may be almost as great as the sense of loss.

Those feelings are compounded further when the individual has chosen to die by his own hand. If social or financial pressures were great upon the individual, these pressures often await solution by the bereaved relatives. This is especially a burden when one is endeavouring to cope with grief in the context of many unresolved family problems.

It is often easier to cope with suicide when one realises that the deceased was genuinely and seriously psychologically ill, whether suffering from depression or other major mental illness. Anger is not an uncommon symptom in bereavement and, sometimes, this anger may be directed against those who were treating the deceased. Research has shown, however, that the act of suicide cannot be predicted even with a modicum of certainty. Suicide is no longer seen as a crime. Those enjoined with responsibility for the treatment of illness may, however, be criticised, usually unfairly, if suicide is the outcome.

The response of some relatives is one of anger directed towards the memory of the deceased. The manner and circumstances of the death may provoke such anger. In taking their own life, the deceased may have sought to tarnish or limit the life of the bereaved. Such situations may result in prolonged distress and disability. An initial or enduring response may be one of numbness and indifference to many aspects of personal, professional and family life. What was important once may now be seen as trivial, and enthusiasm for life may be replaced by a sense of pointlessness and dread.

Reactions may differ where the suicide had already disassociated himself from the mainstream of family life. Some alcoholics and many drug addicts may fall into this category. It may also occur in those suffering from personality disorder and also in the case of some of those suffering from schizophrenia. For the bereaved, in these circumstances, there is the unanticipated knock on the door and subsequent explanation by a sympathetic police officer who may have the disadvantage of not knowing all the circumstances of the death. Furthermore, there may be a request for identification and, later, an invitation to attend the coroner's inquest. Each of these episodes presents its own difficulties.

None, however, equals the distress of being first on the scene of a relative's suicide. Among examples of this are a grandmother who discovered her granddaughter hanging on the back of a bedroom door, a schoolboy who found his father in a fume-filled car and a schoolgirl who found her father hanging in a garage on return from school. The list of tragedy is, apparently, endless. Nevertheless, the resilience of survivors is often remarkable. Some succeed, almost independently, in steering a successful course between the Scylla of callousness and the Charybdis of despondency.

SURVIVOR GUILT IS A well-described phenomenon. An example would be two soldiers exposed to danger where one is killed and the other spared. Contrary to feeling relief, the survivor feels guilty as if he were the person who caused the death of his friend. In suicide, sometimes the parent, spouse or child blames herself or himself for the death. Often this self-blame can reach inordinate levels, and the anger that might have been directed previously in life at the deceased is now turned in upon the self. The hard message is, however, that life must go on, much as a ship's crew must see to the safety of the vessel even when a man has been lost overboard.

Post-traumatic stress disorder has been defined clearly in recent decades. Apart from anxiety and depression, the main symptoms include intrusive thoughts by day and distressing dreams by night. Both the thoughts and the dreams of the suicidally bereaved can be infused with distressing memories of the person who is gone. Occasionally, wish-fulfilment can generate dreams where the lost person appears hale and hearty and as they were years before their death. Wakefulness crushes this escape from pain. So also, by day, thoughts and images may invoke happier times only to be jarred out of the way by unwelcome memories of the manner of the death.

It is not, however, only the past which is a cause for concern. The thought that the future may bring with it the suicide of another relative can distress a person further. There has, in fact, been more than one suicide in some families. It is important to remember, however, that suicide is a comparatively rare phenomenon. The frequency is in the order of one per ten thousand people. The likelihood of two suicides in one family is considerably less than this and may be as low as one per hundred thousand or one per two hundred thousand people. It is less likely to occur if the problem is faced and talked out.

Where depression runs in the family, as it sometimes does, then it is important that each afflicted member gets the necessary treatment. If the extent of the grief is great, and if it is not improving in spite of reflection and discussion with friends and relatives, then it may be appropriate to consider professional help. In previous centuries, priests and ministers of religion offered the rudiments of counselling and psychological support. Over the past century, these roles are increasingly being taken over by medicine and psychologists. Doctors, as part of their training, are given experience in treating psychological illnesses, both with counselling and, where appropriate, with medication. Registered clinical psychologists, and those who have undergone specialist training, are skilled in helping the bereaved to find the path back to sound emotional health. Psychiatrists receive a detailed training in all aspects of emotional illness, both in its medicinal treatment and in its psychotherapy.

In a minority of cases, the level of distress amounts to illness. The symptoms of depressive illness include a prolonged, painful lowering of mood which may be associated with feelings that the world is meaningless, the future is hopeless and the self is worthless. There may be many physiological changes including poor sleeping, difficulty in getting off to sleep, awakening during the night and awakening early, as well as diminution of appetite (sometimes over-eating), change in weight (both a loss and an increase), loss of energy, poor concentration, attenuation of interests, and what doctors call diurnal variation – in other words, profound changes of mood throughout the day, often feeling very poorly in the mornings with improvement towards nightfall, although on occasion the opposite may occur. Occasionally, the bereaved may feel, or become, suicidal. Much more rarely, there are examples of child following father and even more rarely, father following son into suicide. There are also, unfortunately, very uncommon cases where several members of one family have died by suicide. Some of these may be a consequence of example, but others may reflect an underlying biochemical abnormality affecting the metabolism of serotonin and its relationship to other brain chemicals called amines.

Anxiety may be a second common response. Sometimes it occurs alone and, other times, in association with depression. Confidence is lost. Decision-making is difficult, and security within the self and within the social milieu is threatened. Often, physical symptoms break through, including rapid pulse, sweating, palpitations, restlessness and changes in muscle tension which give a sense of physical weakness. If bladder and bowel muscle is affected, there is a social dread of incontinence, so that the individual feels insecure if he does not have immediate access to a lavatory. Open spaces and closed spaces may be a further source of dread. Queuing and waiting become intolerable. Crowds and social gatherings may be perceived as sources of threat to be avoided.

Such conditions require specialist counselling and may also benefit by taking appropriate medication. The giving of medicine is not meant to blur the mind but rather to reduce the length and severity of genuine illness.

NEXT TO ONE'S OWN personality, the most valuable instrument of recovery is one's friends or relatives – if one is fortunate enough to have such genuine persons in one's environment. We are social beings. As explained in the beginning, our personalities emerge from the social world of our parents and siblings. So also, our return to health is likely to be facilitated by secure and trusting relationships.

The great boon of life is a confiding relationship with someone who accepts you as you are, for what you are. In the context of such a relationship, it is possible to work one's way through the greatest disappointments that life can offer. Grieving, like illness, takes time. It cannot be rushed.

Once the sun breaks through, it must be taken as a signal that recovery is possible, even though the sky once more may become overcast and heavy-laden. Unfortunately, personalities differ in the focus of their attention. Those who see the sunlight and remember it do better throughout the dark days than those who are overwhelmed by the greyness and selectively ignore, or forget about, the light.

In a sense, today we are protected from death in a way that our antecedents were not. Most children in Victorian times grew up in the presence of death, either of siblings or of close adult relatives, virtually all of whom would have been nursed and waked at home. This may have had the effect of desensitising them to loss of life. Today, however, death is a much more unusual event, less frequently taking place at home and rarely waked there. The sanitised funeral parlour may have negative psychological effects.

Nevertheless, we are fashioned by nature through many generations to cope with loss and bereavement. If we were not, we could not have survived as a group. Faith in the resourcefulness of our own natures is important in looking towards the future with a genuine sense of biological optimism.

RELATIVES, IN SUICIDE, MAY cope from within their own resources, both of personality and personal contact, or they may cope once given the extra assistance of professional help. Some, however, may need more or may wish to seek an approach which is independent of professional help and independent of everyday social contact. The Friends of the Suicide Bereaved provide such an opportunity. Active groups exist in Cork and Dublin and although they may receive subventions from health boards, they retain control of their own organisation which, as in the case of Alcoholics Anonymous, is essential to their own integrity. They provide a helpline, individual contact and group discussion. They realise that each person's circumstances are different and they refrain from imposing a unitary or standardised response to this highly individualised loss. They listen, gently probe, quietly support and actively affirm individuals in their endeavour to gradually reconstitute themselves as whole individuals.

Since most suicides are male, there is a higher proportion of females amongst the bereaved. All of The Friends of the Suicide Bereaved that I have met to date have been female. This may also reflect the practice of Al-Anon where the majority of members are female, whereas in the case of Alcoholics Anonymous itself, the majority are male. Contact points for The Friends of the Suicide Bereaved are given at the end of this book.

IN SUMMARY, SUICIDE IS a tragedy. A life is ended before its time, in circumstances that are often painful, rarely dignified and virtually always distressing if not patently harmful to the bereaved. Society's response should be better organised and better researched than it has been in Ireland heretofore. In twenty-five years, some 3,000 people were murdered in Northern Ireland. During the same period, at least three times this number, if not four times it, died by suicide in the Republic of Ireland. It would not be expensive to set up a committee of experts to review each case of suicide. At present, the coroners do an excellent job and they would be willing to provide better, more standardised information if requested to do so. The Central Statistics Office has always been most helpful in endeavouring to provide information. There is a need, however, for a concerted effort by the appropriate government departments to clearly delimit the size of the problem, the factors that have led to its increase and the changes most likely to result in curtailment and reduction.

We are a small island with a comparatively small population. Virtually no one in this country is personally untouched by suicide. Each of us who is so affected must look death in the eye if we are to triumph over it. It is best to face the pain which, mercifully for most, diminishes without either medication or professional help. This is as it should be. Tragedies are invariably family affairs. The individual and the family are often better off solving them by themselves. Guilt and blame are not restorative of health. The bereaved should feel grateful if they do not experience either of these two related emotions. The challenge of grieving is to remember the deceased without focusing unduly or painfully on the manner of their death. This is so in all cases of bereavement, but much more so in the case of death by suicide.

Suicide and homicide have something in common. In the one, individuals are killed by someone else and in the other, they take their own life. While many in this country, both north and south, have had to forgive those who have cut human life off before its full course, so also those bereaved by suicide must forgive the deceased and, in doing so, release their own spirit from unhappiness and pain.

STILLBIRTH

DR KEVIN CONNOLLY

IN SOME WAYS A stillbirth is one of the most difficult of deaths to come to terms with. Death before birth, parents outliving their child, little acknowledgement by society of the grief caused by the death – all of these factors can make it very difficult for parents to rationalise the death and work through their grief. And it is not a small problem. Each year, in Ireland, about 300 babies die before birth. This means that 600 parents are bereaved, and a large number of siblings and grandparents also suffer.

A stillbirth is coldly defined as the death of a foetus which weighs at least 500 grams. A fresh stillbirth is one delivered within 1–2 days of death. A macerated stillbirth is one which has been dead for some time, resulting in changes in the baby's skin which can cause the skin to peel off easily during delivery. These terms – fresh or macerated stillbirth – are most inappropriate. They give no acknowledgement to the 'humanness' of the baby or to the fact that there was a life for up to nine months before the baby died.

WHY DO SOME BABIES die before they are born? There are three factors involved in causing stillbirths – abnormalities in the baby, abnormalities of the placenta or afterbirth, and problems in the mother. Problems in the baby which can result in stillbirth are uncommon. They include congenital abnormalities such as major heart problems. One of a pair of twins may die because blood drains from one twin into the other. Sometimes the baby may develop an infection which can cause death in the womb. If the placenta is unhealthy or small, not enough oxygen or nutrients may get to the baby, and if the baby does not get enough fuel, he may die. Finally, some problems of the mother, such as severe hypertension (raised blood pressure), uncontrolled diabetes, or severe kidney problems can cause the death of the baby. It is also known that babies of women who smoke are more at risk of dying both before and after birth. Unfortunately, in a number of cases no cause can be found for the death of the baby.

In order to find out why a baby has died it is necessary to carry out a post-mortem. This is an examination of the baby in an attempt to find out why the baby died, and also to find out if there are any other problems which might recur in a future pregnancy, for instance a heart problem. It may also help doctors prevent such a death in the future. A lot of people fear that a post-mortem involves cutting their baby into small bits, and that they will not be able to see the baby afterwards. Both these fears are without foundation. A post-mortem examination involves an incision of the chest and abdomen, and at the back of the baby's head. When the post-mortem has been finished, these cuts are stitched up and the baby will look the same as before the examination. In every case it should be possible to see and hold your baby after the post-mortem examination.

I very strongly encourage that all babies who die before birth have this examination carried out. From my experience, the majority of people who have not given permission for such an examination regret it in the long-term, as they wish to have as much information about their baby as possible. The preliminary results of the post-mortem should be available straight away, and in the vast majority of cases all results should be back within a few weeks. In a lot of cases no definite cause for the baby's death can be found, particularly if a baby has been dead for some time before birth. This can be difficult for parents because for some people, if a reason for their baby's death has been found, that death may be easier to accept.

A STILLBIRTH IS ONE of the worst tragedies that can befall a couple and has huge after-effects. In order to understand why stillbirth has such an impact on parents and in an effort to help the bereaved to grieve in a healthy way, it is necessary to know the effects that pregnancy has on a woman, to know the factors that can affect the grief which occurs after a stillbirth, and to know of simple interventions which can help affect the mourning process. It is very important also to know the usual grief reactions.

Pregnancy is a *developmental milestone*, when a woman becomes a mother. This change into a mother can help establish a more secure and independent sense of adult identity. Her new identity as a mother is negotiated with those around her, for instance by attending antenatal clinics, buying maternity clothes, and so on. A stillbirth, therefore, can result in a crisis within a crisis. The mother is very vulnerable, and thus has much need for social support from available, empathic and helpful people. The desire to get pregnant quickly, and the mental pain experienced when seeing and hearing another person's baby, may be due to this interference in developmental progress, as well as being a result of the death of the baby. This pain may be particularly marked if it is a couple's first child who has died. One couple recently told me that they had bought a pram, a cot, clothes and nappies, and now they had no use for them.

A second aspect of pregnancy is that of *enhancement of a woman's self-image*. She has planned to produce the ideal child, endowed with her own best qualities and with those she would like to have had. A considerable portion of her self-esteem is invested in the future child – she feels power because she has created a child, and she is confirming her femininity by becoming a mother. When death occurs in pregnancy, many of the usual responses – emptiness, low self-esteem and unbearable helplessness – result from a mother's feeling that she has lost a part of herself, so this sense of helplessness is understandable. An underlying feeling of shame and inferiority, which can be caused by this injury to herself, may be particularly painful.

A third aspect of pregnancy is the development of an *intense attachment* by the parent towards the unborn child. This attachment occurs gradually through the pregnancy and usually occurs much earlier in the mother than in the father. The amount of grief experienced is related to the strength of attachment which has developed towards the unborn baby. Some men do not develop an attachment to the baby until

113

very late in pregnancy or until after their child is born. This may mean that these fathers will have less of a grief reaction than the mother has.

A VERY IMPORTANT PART of any mourning is the recalling of memories we have of the dead person – both happy and sad memories. When death occurs in pregnancy, mourning is complicated by lack of memories of the baby. This may be further compounded by lack of professional and familial support and by the unexpected suddenness of death. Some mothers doubt the reality both of the pregnancy and of the death of their baby. Some do not accept that their baby has died until the baby is born and they see no life. For some, it can be weeks after the burial of their baby before the fact of the death fully sinks in. As a person will not start to work through the grief until he or she accepts that the baby is dead, I very strongly encourage parents to take every opportunity to establish the reality of the dead child so that mourning their baby can be facilitated. Naming, seeing, holding, and burying one's dead child can significantly help the mourning. So also can the funeral and burial service.

A funeral serves a number of functions. It makes the death real for parents, siblings, family and friends. It allows the bereaved the opportunity to express their grief. It gives social support to the bereaved, and it helps friends to express their feelings. In the case of a stillbirth there may be no ritual service or no burial. The absence of either of these implies that the baby wasn't really worth a Mass or a decent funeral and can give the message to parents that it is only a 'little' death, so little grieving is necessary. Also, in attempts to help, people say things like 'You weren't really pregnant', 'Wouldn't it be worse if he had lived for a while?', 'Haven't you got other children?', or 'Can't you have more?' These statements are telling the bereaved indirectly that they should not really be upset. As a result, the parents may not talk about the death. However, feelings of sorrow, loss, anger, guilt and fear must be expressed in order for grief to be worked through.

So parents will grieve, though to a different extent, after

a stillbirth. How this grief proceeds is affected by a number of factors. The personality of the bereaved has the greatest influence on how that person grieves. The way we respond to death is determined, to a large extent, by the way our parents responded to our attachment behaviour during infancy and childhood. If our parents were available, responsive and helpful we will not mind showing our helplessness. We will be able to look for support and will be able to develop a plan to help us through our grief. If, on the other hand, we experienced an unsympathetic attitude to our needs for love and affection, or if the expression of feelings like sadness and disappointment was frowned on, we may find it difficult to express our grief, and are more likely to have a disordered grief reaction.

The circumstances of the baby's death can affect grief. If a mother has had a large vaginal bleed (an antepartum haemorrhage) she may fear that she will die. If her worries that something was wrong with her baby were dismissed, she will naturally suffer anger if the baby subsequently dies. If the baby was born at home, parents may wonder if they could have revived their baby. If the mother had an infection, she may blame the infection for the baby's death. The use of sedatives and sleeping tablets can subdue the immediate grief reaction, can dim the memory of the event, and may increase guilt by implying to the parents that being upset is not normal. It is only in very rare cases that such sedative drugs should be used.

THE WAY MEN DEAL with their grief differs to that of women. There are many reasons for this. While a boy is growing up, he learns how to behave by copying his parents, teachers, relatives and friends. He assumes a male role which, in general, is very helpful. However, it can inhibit healthy grieving. One role is that of the macho-man. This starts early on and is reinforced by statements such as 'Good man, you didn't cry'. By the time we are adults it is assumed that crying is showing a weakness. Therefore, if a man is hurt in any way, he does not cry. In the event of death how then can a man let out his sadness? He can find it particu-

115

larly difficult to cry in the presence of another male. The tears, therefore, are suppressed. He will turn his mind to something else and this only postpones, rather than gets rid of, his grief. It can also cause him to become irritable and angry, and less able to support his partner. As a result of this, his partner may feel either that he doesn't care or that he doesn't understand how she is feeling. This can lead to large stress in their relationship. Society can also make it difficult for a man to express his grief – comments like 'You are great the way you are coping', reinforce the expectation that men should not cry.

Give sorrow words; the grief that does not speak
Knits up the o'erwrought heart and bids it break.

Shakespeare

After a stillbirth there is no paternity leave. Fathers often have to return to work outside the home soon after a baby's death and long before the initial stage of grief has been worked through. Most of his workmates will find it difficult to bring up the topic of the death and will talk about anything other than the dead baby. The father may become deeply engrossed in his work and may spend longer time away from home. This may be partly to avoid returning home to face the distress of his grieving wife. Throughout this time, the mother is faced each day with reminders of her grief, and emotionally is much better able to work through her feelings either by talking to her friends or by crying. So while her grief is proceeding, the father's grief may be blocked.

Most men need to feel self-sufficient. They tend to believe that this means being able to cope no matter what the circumstances. In the situation when his child has died, he may continue to say he is well when asked how things are and may find it particularly difficult to share his feelings with his neighbours or friends. Men may find it very difficult to accept professional help, as this implies that they depend on somebody and dependence is not an acceptable masculine trait.

It is important to remember that some men may feel little or no sense of loss if their baby dies, particularly if the death has occurred early on in pregnancy. This absence of a feeling of loss is because some men do not become attached to their baby until late in pregnancy or indeed, in some cases, until after their child has been born. So if no attachment has developed, no sense of loss will be experienced. This can bother the father if he thinks he should be grieving even though he feels no sense of loss, and it can bother his partner if although she is grieving, he seems not to care.

CHILDREN CAN BE VERY deeply affected by the death of their baby brother or sister, even if they only felt their mother's swollen abdomen or the movements of the baby in the womb and did not know the baby alive outside the womb. Even though they may not have been told directly that a baby was expected or that the baby has died, they will know that something major has happened. Because of this, they too need to grieve. However, it can be very difficult for parents who are going through their own grief to know how to help their children.

In the same way as there is no one right grief reaction in parents, children react differently to death. Their reaction depends on their personality, on their age, on their parents' reactions and on their previous experience of talking about or dealing with death. Very young children are well aware when their parents are upset, and it is a mistake to try and conceal your distress or conceal the fact that the baby has died. It is also a mistake to send a child away to a friend or a relation. At a time of grief and upset, children need the comfort of their parents' presence. Children should be given an opportunity to see their dead brother or sister, even though you may be advised not to allow this. People may say it will upset them too much. However, the death usually *will* upset the child and it is far better that children are allowed show their distress than have to bottle it up. Children also should be allowed put things like a teddy bear or soother into the coffin, and they should be given photographs of the dead baby to keep.

Children show their grief in different ways. Younger children, in some ways, are far better than older children because they are much more open to asking questions like 'Why is he so cold?', 'Why don't you put a hot-water bottle in?', 'When he dies in Heaven will he come back to earth?' Older children may tend not to mention the death and we may mistakenly think they are not affected by it because they do not talk about it. However, this is not so. Like some adults, they may try to suppress/bury their too-painful thoughts and feelings. They may not talk in case they will upset their parents. They may not have been involved in talk about the dead baby, and may have taken this as a cue that they should not bring up the subject of death.

Very young children who cannot verbalise their grief may develop behaviour problems such as temper tantrums, sleeping difficulties, bowel or bladder problems, or excess clinging. If these behaviour problems are handled in a sensitive fashion they should not result in long-term difficulties. They can, however, cause ongoing problems if they are mismanaged. There is good evidence that if parents accept their children's grief and if they facilitate the child's expression of this grief, then their children will be able to handle grief in a healthy way.

HOW DO PEOPLE REACT when they learn their child has died? It is one of the most shattering things a person can ever be told. The shock may completely numb a person's feelings, so that they may appear either not to have heard or not to react. Or they may get completely distraught and agitated. And some may initially react as if nothing has happened. Each of these reactions is normal and is that person's way of coping in the initial period of their shock.

There is a huge array of feelings which occur after this shock phase. One of the first is denial. 'Surely the doctor is wrong?', 'Couldn't they do the scan again?', 'Maybe the machine doesn't work properly?' Some do not fully accept the death until their baby is born. There can be a lot of anger – anger at the nurse who tells them their baby is dead, anger at the doctor who should have delivered the baby while he was still alive, anger at God. 'Why should He let our baby die when we have not done anything wrong and we really wanted our baby?' Anger at the partner. 'Why did he insist on making love the week before the movements stopped?' Anger at self. 'Why did I put off getting pregnant for so long?', 'Why didn't I stop working?', 'Why did I keep on smoking?' It is very important to realise that these feelings of anger are normal and that they must be expressed. Otherwise the grief may be blocked. If these feelings of anger are not sorted out and worked through, grief may not proceed normally.

After the initial reaction of anger, denial, guilt and confusion comes the phase of sadness. This can be very intense. There may be sudden depths of sadness causing uncontrollable crying, occurring out of the blue. Or the tears may come after reminders of the dead baby – nappies in a shop, seeing someone else's baby, passing the hospital, the day of the week that the baby died, and so on. The day that the baby was due may be particularly difficult. These pangs of sadness can continue for months, but as the grief proceeds they occur less often. It is very important to let the tears come and particularly not to hide them from the other children or friends. Crying is important in helping the work of grief. It also helps others realise it is right and good to cry.

It can be very difficult meeting people after such a tragedy. The bereaved will not know what to say and people may either cross the road to avoid meetings, or they may talk about the weather, the match, the government, anything except the dead baby. But even though it is very upsetting to bring up the subject, the bereaved almost always want to talk and talk about what has happened. Not talking about it will only postpone the grieving. It is impossible to say how long the grieving will last, how long it will take until a day might go by without thinking about the baby, until thinking about the baby doesn't cause tears, until the thoughts are wistful rather than sad. All this can take months and months. Even though you are always bereaved and will never get over it, you learn to live with it.

THE HANDLING OF STILLBIRTH by hospital staff has improved markedly in the last twenty years. This change has, to a large extent, been brought about by groups such as the Irish Stillbirth and Neonatal Death Society. There is much more appreciation on the part of doctors, nurses and the clergy that bereaved parents need to grieve, that as many memories as possible must be provided to the bereaved family and that statements such as 'Forget about it, and get on with your life', show enormous insensitivity and lack of insight.

Of course it is upsetting for a doctor or a nurse to have to tell parents their baby is dead – it is difficult to know what to say, it is very disquieting to be faced with angry, crying, accusing parents. Doctors feel very uncomfortable in a passive role and many feel very awkward when trying to comfort shocked parents. Doctors can also experience a feeling of failure in not having ensured that a woman gives birth to a live, healthy baby. The nurse who first suspects that a baby whose heartbeat she is looking for is in fact dead, may never have been taught how to cope in this situation. And, like the doctor, she may not know the normal immediate grief reactions. Some doctors seem to be incapable of coping with this very stressful situation. A lot of doctors find it difficult to admit that they do not know everything. Parents may feel that the doctor should have been able to prevent their baby from dying, or should have delivered the baby sooner. They may have been told in an insensitive fashion that their baby had died. The hospital staff may find it difficult to talk about the death and about parents' feelings because they themselves are upset. The job of a doctor or midwife in a maternity ward is to make sure that a healthy baby is born. If a baby dies before or after birth, the medical staff may feel that they have failed in their duty.

Some people are much better than others at helping the bereaved in this situation. Some people are by nature much better at comforting those who are crying or who are upset. Some are better at consoling. And some find it very difficult to cope with other people's distress. Some doctors forget that people do not understand technical terms or long medical words. Care can fall between a number of stools – the obstetrician may feel his job is finished, the paediatrician has no baby to look after, and nurses may not know whether the mother should be in the antenatal ward, the postnatal ward, or away from babies altogether. Parents may meet many different people and get conflicting information and advice. Doctors may opt out of meeting bereaved parents if there are pastoral care workers, social workers, clergy or bereavement counsellors to help the bereaved. But as one person has said 'We do not necessarily need a new profession of bereavement counsellors. We do need more thought, sensitivity and activity concerning this issue on the part of the existing professional groups.' Parents may focus their anger on the doctor, who in his distress may find it difficult to accept that anger. He may distance himself from parents or get angry and defensive, rather than allow parents to express and work through their anger. We must remember that this anger is a normal, reasonable reaction. After all, if God is good, why did He allow this tragedy to happen?

Anyone dealing with parents of a stillborn baby should know the usual grief reactions. All should realise that although a lot of feelings are commonly experienced, everyone's grief is unique. Parents must be facilitated so that they can express their grief in their own way. This requires adaptability and flexibility on the part of hospital staff.

No one can take in all that is said to them the first time they hear it – they may need to be told over and over again. Bereaved parents want accurate, understandable information about what happened and why it may have happened. Most people do not understand technical or medical terms. They need sensitive guidance about what they need to do. This means that hospital staff should know details about different funeral rituals, about how to direct people regarding burial arrangements, about registration of the stillbirth, and so on. In this situation particularly, parents must be treated with respect, their feelings must be accepted even if their anger and distress is upsetting, and they must be given information in a clear fashion. This information may need to be repeated, as it is impossible to take in everything we are told when we are in a state of shock. The following are some questions parents may ask, and hospital staff dealing with these parents must know how to answer them.

- How and why did our baby die?
- Was it our fault?
- What does a post-mortem involve, when will we get the results, and who will tell us?
- Can we see and hold and dress the baby after the post-mortem?
- Can the baby's brothers, sisters, aunts see the baby?
- What mementos can we get – photographs, name-tags, footprints, the baby's measurements, a lock of hair? Remember, one of the most important memories is time spent with the dead baby.
- How do we arrange for a religious service and for the burial? When should we do this? Remember that the bereaved may find it difficult to make decisions at this time. But they should be allowed to decide and they should not be rushed.
- How should we expect to feel?
- Who will talk to us about our grief reactions?
- What sort of help will we need? Remember to arrange follow-up appointments and to get the booklet, *A Little Lifetime*, which discusses immediate arrangements, grief reactions and sources of help (see Further Reading).
- Could it happen again?
- When should we try to have another baby? Remember it is difficult to greet our next baby until we have said farewell to the baby who has died.

As time goes by and as the grief proceeds, parents are able to look ahead. Days go by when they do not think of the baby. When they do think and talk about the baby there may be no tears, but a wistful sadness. At this stage, parents are slowly letting go of their baby. This does not mean stopping loving

122

the baby. It means putting the baby in a special place in their memory, it means moving on, it means being able to think of developing another attachment. But even though grief will eventually be worked through, we must always remember that the brief life was unique and very important and that the impact of a stillbirth causes a huge scar which takes a long time to heal.

DEATH BY MURDER

JOHN DONOHOE

IN OUTLINING WHAT THE experience of grief following the murder of a loved one might be like, I have one aim in mind. I do not wish to convince you of my point of view. Nor do I wish to provide answers. Rather, I only hope to provoke you to think, and evaluate for yourself what this experience might be like. What is it like to be bereaved by the death of someone you care about, knowing that the death came about by murder? Nothing will, or can, prepare you for the experience of intense and prolonged emotional distress or the exacerbation of this distress by the processes which are meant to help you. The comments here are based on my clinical experience in working with many families bereaved in this way. Also, theory and research in the field have contributed many valuable insights. Initially, I will define what I mean by grief, and how it affects you on different levels. I will then go on to outline the specific features that make bereavement through murder distinctive.

Here I am defining grief as one's reaction experience to being left behind. It is the internal experience of what it is like to be left bereaved after the murder of someone you love and care about. By bereaved, I mean to lose someone through death. To me, this experience is unique. When we are bereaved it touches us in a most personal way. It touches us subjectively, in that we know that we too will die. And it touches us objectively, because we are attached to the deceased – therefore, we will miss them. We will miss what is specific to them, hence grief brings out in us the totality of our humanity. No other experience comes close to grief. All forms of grief are similar, in that they are spread across the same dimensions. However, the grief subsequent to a murder is quite distinctive, because of the many specific features particular to it.

Because grief impacts itself on the total person, we need to describe it in a way that encompasses what a person is. This is very difficult, as you can imagine. So I have tried to do this by elaborating what I see as seven general dimensions by which we describe ourselves and our grief. These seven dimensions are as follows:

EMOTIONAL: Probably the one that most of us would consider first when we try to describe what grief is. Certainly, the emotions are the most immediate dimension of grief. Well, where does one start trying to describe this dimension? The hundreds of possible emotions that can be experienced in grief are very often overwhelming and defeating. Typically one feels shock, numbness, sadness, despair, loneliness, anger, guilt, outrage, confusion, yearning, pining, anxiety, relief, helplessness, hopelessness, vulnerable, sentimental, and so on. There are many, many feelings. In passing, I wish to comment on only one feature of the emotional dimension – that of ambivalence. This is the experience of feeling conflicting emotions towards the same person, event or object at the same time. This emotional dilemma can create enormous difficulties for people, because they have to try to ventilate the conflicting sides of their emotions. It is this feature which often prevents adequate adjustment by the individual to their bereavement. Particular to bereavement by murder, one often experiences an overwhelming sense of guilt – 'Could I have prevented it?', 'Why didn't I do more?', etc. There is also the inexpressible rage which is provoked by so many aspects of the experience – the injustice, the form of death, the way it is handled by the legal bodies, etc.

COGNITIVE: Does anything happen in our lives to which our thinking does not react? The myriad of thoughts which we can go through in grief is like Joyce's 'streams of consciousness' in *Ulysses*, often illogical, strange, bizarre, questioning, etc., but never without reason or purpose. But to understand the reason or purpose is, of course, the difficulty. Why are we so preoccupied with the deceased? Why does our ability to concentrate deteriorate? Why does our ability to be attentive diminish, why does our memory seem to be so frustratingly affected? Why do we get confused? Why do we dream so distressingly? And so on go the descriptive questions which the clinician hears.

And often, for this group of people, the awful thoughts and imaginings centre around the moments of dying. What did the deceased experience consciously? What went through their minds as they died?

BEHAVIOURAL: Just by becoming bereaved, you take part in novel behaviour such as ritual mourning, wearing black, entertaining lots of people for a few weeks and then entertaining none, going up to the grave at all sorts of times, going back into the room that the deceased lay in, having to do tasks which the deceased previously used to do, and so on. The behavioural changes involved in grief are often distressing, and reluctantly carried out or patently avoided. Either way they constitute a large part of the grieving individual's experiences.

PHYSICAL: Any grieving individual will tell you that grief is so like illness – how heavy their heart feels, how their body is reacting to this number one stressor. Symptoms include palpitations, tightness in the chest, migraine, headaches, skin rashes, tiredness and fatigue, gastric and bowel upsets. These somatic features are now more readily accepted in this stress-conscious age, so I do not need to elaborate further here.

SOCIAL: As soon as you become bereaved and start grieving, you begin to behave differently towards others. Either you huddle together as a family, or you start avoiding each other and other people because you just cannot deal with them, or are afraid of getting hurt. So also do they relate differently towards you, at one time openly coming towards you, later avoiding you, or talking to you as though the death has not occurred.

The media focus and the enormous crowds which often turn up to a funeral following a murder, are very distressing, stressful additions to the grief following murder.

SPIRITUAL: Does God exist? Why did He take my child? What use is the priest, rabbi or spiritual leader to me, when all I want is my child back? Or alternatively 'Only for my faith I couldn't have coped'. Either way, the significance of spiritual dimensions is apparent. Other questions about sins, afterlife, and contact with the deceased are also often features of this dimension.

PHILOSOPHICAL: What is the meaning of life? What sense can I make of the three week-old life of a foetus lost through ectopic pregnancy? What of justice or evil, what role do they have? Why should I not commit suicide also? These may not seem like the more immediate features of grief, but they are the ones which often sustain the grief for many years. What is the meaning of my loved one's life? How can I make sense of someone, often a stranger, needlessly killing my son, daughter, brother, sister, mother, father or partner? What about justice for me or my family? These perplexing and justifiable questions aggravate the bereaved considerably.

FOLLOWING ON FROM THESE seven dimensions in which grief is experienced, it is worth outlining the different ways in which the individual is personally challenged by death. For descriptive purposes, this section is divided into three levels. Each level has a distinctive sense of its own. Yet they are interrelated. How the individual meets the challenges on one level will influence how he meets them on another. Also, all three levels are experienced through the seven dimensions.

LEVEL I. Grieving the Deceased: This level has to do with the bereaved's relationship to the deceased, and how the bereaved will respond to the realisation that the relationship has irrevocably changed, now that one side of the relationship is gone The bereaved has to adapt to the world with the deceased missing. They will not 'get over' the bereavement. Rather, they will learn to adapt. This level is what most people consider grief to be about, i.e., their getting over the ending of the relationship to the deceased.

LEVEL II. Grieving Yourself: We are not concerned only with the bereaved's relationship to the deceased. We must also take into account how the death, especially through murder, influences the individual's experience of themselves. When someone you love has been the victim of murder, you the bereaved become victimised as well. Being involved in death is a traumatic experience and we cannot remain indifferent. That part of us that is constituted by the deceased, dies as well. It is murdered too. Something inside us dies.

Also we are reminded that some day we too will die. Our own mortality becomes a vulnerability which unnerves us and underpins our grief. In this way we are drawn, all of us, to all deaths. And following a bereavement in this way, it becomes impossible to deny or ignore death any longer.

LEVEL III. The Destruction of Our Belief System: How can we ever have the same belief about life, about ourselves again? To the point that we once believed, we now consider it irrelevant in the extreme to do so now. Our former beliefs are not in touch with our newly realised reality.

We cannot believe we were so innocent about life – that life which is good, fair, and just, where nothing terribly bad will happen to us or our loved ones.

We realise that we believed we were in control of most things in our life, and that we would be in control should we ever be bereaved. We believed that we would cope with anything life threw at us. Now we feel that this notion of control is a myth, a construct for reassurance. We don't feel in control of the lives of the deceased, or of our own. We feel that even our grief is out of control.

We believed that assurance and expectation were reasonable ways of looking at things, and now these seem vacuous and useless. This loss of belief causes us to feel anxious, depressed, even at times suicidal. We wish that it were all different. We hope that somehow we will wake up to find that this whole reality has been a nightmare. Often it is at this point that our religious faith plays a part. And, if so, then the individual may feel considerably less distress. But we may also view our faith as another belief-system which no longer holds true. Hence we may come to think and feel that there are no beliefs worth upholding.

The third and final level is an existential battle – a battle in our own minds about the very quality of our existence, about the existence of everybody.

It lacks the objectivity of the first level and the subjectivity of the second level. It goes beyond both, to centre on the meaning of life, on the meaning of the deceased's life, on the meaning of your own life, and ultimately on the meaning of all our lives. How one answers these questions for oneself is central to any resolution one may achieve in one's grief. I will return to this later.

So now, having looked at how grief is defined and constituted irrespective of the type of death, let us look at the distinctive features of grief following murder.

THE NATURE OF THE death and how the victim was murdered is of central importance. Was it particularly violent? Was it the act of an insane person? Was it, to some degree, accidental? Was there a sexual dimension? Underlying these types of questions lies a very difficult question and answer for the bereaved person. What did their loved one go through consciously before death? How much did they suffer? It is this which makes murder such a difficult grief to bear. To contend with the deceased's suffering is almost unbearable. At times it can almost seem harder to contend with than the murder. This difficulty can be further exacerbated by the meaninglessness of the violence, the suddenness, and your inability to prepare at all. Also, if you have survived, there can be survivor guilt, the 'If only I had ...' syndrome. This awful self-torturous attack can go on for years. It rests on the failure to see that you, the bereaved, are victims of the murderer too.

ONCE THE MURDER HAS been committed the legal system, the gardaí, the forensic team, the barristers, the state pathologist, the defence teams, become involved. The state owns the body of the deceased and, in principle, the evidence as well! These two features, the involvement of intermediaries and the withholding of the reality, are what make this type of bereavement and the ensuing grief so difficult. *Your* loved one, the person you may have shared so much of your life with, is the deceased. Now *you* have no control over the body. *You* cannot prevent the autopsy. *You* cannot know all the details of the death. This is the second taking. The murderer took the life. The system takes away your chance to integrate the reality into yourself.

Other exacerbating features experienced through the legal system include how the murderer is charged, whether they are fit to plead, whether the charge is sustained as murder or manslaughter, whether they plead guilty or not guilty? Also, occasionally during an investigation, relatives of the deceased may be questioned, come under suspicion, even be charged, only later to be released. This type of experience could easily be appreciated as a cause of inexpressible rage.

And so it goes, the experience of being bereaved through murder, being exacerbated by the conventions of the legal system.

THE OFTEN INTENSE FOCUS by television, radio and newspapers can be very distressing. To be besieged for details about the deceased, about the death and about the family history, is a further assault on the senses. To top this, speculations, inaccuracies and sensationalism are commonplace. Furthermore, details of the death may be revealed for the first time by the media. This can adversely affect normal family communications, with detrimental effects on the family's system of mutual support. The media can have a beneficial value, but they can also aggravate the situation.

IT IS NOT UNCOMMON for people bereaved in this way to develop psychiatric problems, such as depression, anxiety and phobic reactions, alcoholism, suicidal behaviour, and post-traumatic stress disorder. These problems, in them-

130

selves, can be very distressing, and coming on top of the bereavement and all that goes with it, we can appreciate why the experience is so devastating. Yet specialist services are generally not available. Also, a lot of people bereaved in this way have difficulty in finding adequate interventions. This is also the case in the counselling services. Specialist counselling services for bereavement by murder are only now being developed in this country.

And so, in some cases, the bereaved may feel abandoned by the very services that they may have thought would have helped them. Also, the effects of the symptoms described above can really make the bereaved feel very isolated, misunderstood, and alone in their experience.

WHEN YOUR LOVED ONE is murdered, there is something about it which draws people's interest and attention to it. There may be a fascination with the actions of the murderer, or compassion generated by identifying with your suffering in your bereavement. Either way, upon becoming bereaved through murder, you become swamped by public attention. And whenever you are surrounded by large groups of people, you will be subjected to support, stigmatisation, spectacle, gossip, anger and sympathy. Apart from having to contend with phenomenally large numbers of people, and all that that entails, you also have to contend with everything they might say or do to you. This can be extremely distressing, and later on, having been such a centre of attention, you find that you are now alone and that can be equally bewildering.

SO, AS WE CONSIDER and describe influences from these different groups, we realise that the bereaved person is not only a victim of the murder, but he can inadvertently be further victimised by these groups. The effects of all this on the bereaved family have elsewhere been described as 'the second death', the death of the family.

Also, within the family, the pressures brought about by individual reactions to the death, and having to tolerate these often contrasting differences, can be very difficult. This

131

is because the differences appear to indicate how the family is falling apart. And some family members, in wishing to resist this indication, will not tolerate any signs of the differences being expressed. Feelings of not wanting to talk about it because it is so distressing to do so, combine with these differences to create friction between family members. The only way of overcoming these difficulties is for the family to learn to accommodate the differences, not seeing them as differences, rather seeing them as further contributions about how to cope with the death of the deceased or the ensuing grief.

In essence, the bereaved are left to cope with the murder of someone they loved and with the often severe stresses brought upon them by the involvement of the agencies involved with the murder. To counteract this distressing reality, they have one significant thing going for them – the impact of the deceased's life on their own and everything that the deceased brought to them whilst they were alive. The love, the memories, the relationship, and so on, will constitute the consolation for their grief. It is not the creativity, or productivity, or duration of a life that matters most. Rather it is the impact of one life on another that matters. This is what we grieve. And it is the juxtaposition of this impact against the impact of the death and its aftermath, which determines the grief reaction. How the family supports each member, achieving their own sense of this balance, is the marker for how well the family will cope with the death through murder of someone they love.

DEATH BY CHOICE

NUALA HARMEY

WITHDRAWING INVASIVE TREATMENT FROM a dying patient is an ethical dilemma faced by healthcare professionals, whether doctors, nurses, social workers or chaplains. No one person or profession should have the monopoly in decision-making. Nor can the patient or relatives be excluded from the process. All concerned bring individual value systems to this decision: therefore, all are moral agents with rights as well as obligations. The more people that are involved in the decision-making, the more disagreements on sincerely-held ethical issues that are likely to emerge. However, a healthcare team which is able to acknowledge these differences, is also likely to feel unthreatened by acknowledging the patient's right to be included in the discussion.

Withdrawing treatment is an emotive issue, the contemplation of which can cause great emotional and intellectual distress to well-motivated and concerned professionals. Is there a difference between stopping treatment and never starting it or between withdrawing a treatment and actively assisting death? The resolution of these questions without doing violence to anyone's conscience is vital if we are to achieve a dignified death for our terminally-ill patients.

THERE ARE CERTAIN PRINCIPLES propounded by the major religions which underlie much current medical ethical thinking. Judaism is very often used as a model for discussing ethical issues on terminating treatment as it is accepted as being very firm and coherent on these issues. The Rabbinical tradition accepts that there is a difference in *acting* to end someone's life and *omitting* to do everything possible to save it. Buddhism also judges actions, not in themselves but

133

in their motives. Indeed, differentiating between 'acts' and 'omissions' is basic to many religious and moral codes.

The concept of a 'good death' has also exercised minds throughout the centuries. Changing religious beliefs, medical technology and social attitudes have contributed to a radical re-evaluation of the concept and its interpretation. Very often, those professing religious beliefs have postulated that the opportunity to review one's life and make appropriate amends before dying would constitute a 'good death'.

Belief in a God who needs appeasement before death is not now widely held. The holistic psychotherapeutic approach which may be secular in origin, and the hospice-type philosophy which in many cases has a Christian orientation, also place an emphasis on allowing people to prepare for death. The key element in both these approaches is 'choice'. It is the patient who decides either to avoid the subject or to 'open up' in whatever manner is appropriate to them. This decision is not reached because of any authoritarian dictates of inflexible religious beliefs.

WHEN A CHILD IS the dying patient, the issue of patient autonomy and participation in decision-making becomes a very real dilemma. Many doctors operate on the basis that parents will carry a burden of guilt if they make a decision to terminate their child's treatment.

This motivation may appear to be in the patient's best interests but, in reality, is depriving them of autonomy. An experienced team, dealing with a terminally-ill child and the family, will recognise that parents have an in-depth knowledge of their child – including the child's understanding of the illness, expectations of life, ability to withstand further treatment and their emotional resilience.

Parents dealing with a child's life-threatening illness are operating with a distinct disadvantage in relation to medical staff. Apart from their emotional stress, additional issues and burdens such as disruption of family life, demands of other children, and financial pressures decimate their decision-making ability and make them more vulnerable.

Parents often experience a sense of helplessness and lack

of control in a hospital environment. This, allied to high-technology medicine, undermines their ability to ask questions essential to their understanding and ability to make decisions.

Any approach which does not recognise these issues deprives parents of their legitimate rights. It should also be acknowledged that skilled professionals can discuss issues of life and death in a meaningful way with older children and adolescents and establish a rapport within which their desires regarding further treatment can be established.

DEALING WITH THE DYING and their families as individuals is the key to a 'good death' and a concept worth striving towards. The following case-history illustrates how it can be achieved by combining accurate family knowledge with support and sensitive professional reaction.

A fifteen year-old boy, Bob, has relapsed following a bone marrow transplant. His initial reaction to the knowledge of relapse is one of anger. This is followed by a period of weeks in which he lives very fully and does not mention the disease.

His awareness of his situation is shown by remarks such as 'The point of taking tablets is only to avoid getting a bad rash' or 'There is no point in resting in bed, this tiredness won't be cured by resting'. His family acknowledged the truth of these remarks while not pushing for further discussion.

It had been assumed by all that Bob would die at home. However, five days before his death he remarked to the hospital social worker: 'We (meaning himself, his parents and two brothers) need more time together, there are too many people calling here'.

A discussion between Bob, his parents and siblings, and the social worker followed regarding the advisability of hospital admission, where the family felt the hospital staff could restrict visitors and protect what they perceived as their need for privacy. This was arranged and he died four days later in the presence of his parents and siblings with minimal hospital presence.

Although Bob did not directly discuss his death, he orchestrated the surroundings in which it took place and the manner which was most acceptable to his family. The medical and paramedical response illustrates the necessity of an individual flexible approach.

MODERN HEALTHCARE PROVIDES A broader-based team than doctors and nurses. Social workers, pastoral care workers, counsellors and others are now seen as integral to the process of providing full patient care. The following case-history illustrates how a full team assessment, together with parental involvement and listening to the child patient, led to a decision to withdraw treatment.

Andrew, aged nine, suffered from spina bifida and was paraplegic. The family had provided a warm, caring environment for the child, as had the working class community in which they lived.

There were four other siblings. The eldest, aged twenty, was epileptic. Andrew was functioning at the level of mild mental handicap and had communication difficulties – although within his family circle he could communicate well. He had innumerable hospitalisations since birth and was becoming increasingly more distressed on each hospitalisation.

Andrew's renal function disimproved and the decision to commence dialysis, with eventual kidney transplant, had to be made. Because of other medical complications the success rate for transplant was about five per cent, and dialysis would have meant prolonged and frequent hospitalisation.

The parents were involved in all discussions and they made the decision that he could not cope with further emotional or physical stress. The medical and paramedical teams fully and verbally supported them, having weighed the benefits of possible transplant against the known burden of treatment, with regard also being paid to the autonomy of the parents and child.

Andrew told his mother that he 'Did not want more medicine because it was not going to make him better'. Asked what he wanted, he replied, 'To stay at home and not go back to hospital'.

Active treatment in the form of medication ceased and he died at home four weeks later. The hospital team supported the parents and continued to affirm them in their decision.

SPECIAL SKILLS ARE REQUIRED in assessing children's needs during the terminal phase of their illness. There are techniques for assessing pain and promoting effective management. But the following short case-history will illustrate other factors of equal importance.

Jennifer, a seven year-old only child, was in the terminal phase of a malignant disease. Discussion with the parents showed that the appropriate medication was not being given to Jennifer in the dosage prescribed, despite clear instruction.

The issue that needed to be addressed by the symptom control team was the father's fear of morphine, which to him meant acknowledging that the disease was terminal. The mother feared that regular doses of medication would leave nothing for the last stages, which she assumed would be intractably painful.

Often, parents have to deal emotionally with the impending death of their child before they can dispense accurately opiate pain-relief. Once Jennifer's parents had been helped to accept the reality of her situation, palliative care treatment was successful in helping the child to die well.

PALLIATIVE CARE SHOULD BE viewed as an active branch of medicine offering caring support for terminally-ill persons and their families, whatever the disease involved. It has been viewed as the 'nothing left to do' school of care, when active treatment is of no avail. Nothing could be further from the truth.

The World Health Organisation has defined palliative care as the 'active total care of patients whose disease no longer responds to curative treatment, and for whom the goal must be the best quality of life for them and their families'. The achievement of this goal requires professional skills of as high an order as those displayed in other fields of medicine.

The salient components of palliative care are relief of unpleasant symptoms and enhancing the quality of life remaining to each patient. Integral to this approach is the recognition of the individuality of each person by acknowledging the absolute importance of their psychological, spiritual, social, sexual and physical dimensions.

'The focus of palliative care is to enable dying people to be pain-free, dignified and lucid during the terminal phase of illness. The aim of any treatment used is not to prolong life but to make it as comfortable as possible. The dying person is central to this process and encouraged to retain control as long as is feasible.'[1]

To meet the myriad needs of the dying and their families a team approach is essential, as no one professional is equipped to deal with all the issues. Also the emotional stress imposed on carers, regardless of their professional status, requires the support of a team structure.

The alleviation of pain and other distressing physical symptoms is quite properly regarded as one of the major achievements of palliative care. For symptom control to be effective, the patient must be central to the entire discussion of symptoms and their importance to him or her. The techniques of pain-relief and amelioration of other physical symptoms such as anorexia and weakness cannot be discussed in this essay but are an integral part of palliative care.

It is important to remember that psychological problems cause additional stresses, anxiety and fear. These can be expressed as physical pain. Very often, patients complain of physical symptoms, but careful and compassionate communication may elicit fears and anxieties relating to the disease, to the act of dying or to separation from loved ones.

Social problems such as housing, state benefits, the availability of mobility aids can cause anxiety. Spiritual problems, even in those with no formal religious beliefs, can

---

1. *Open University Workbook 3*, Part 3, Section 8.1, The Open University, Milton Keynes, 1994.

cause great pain. To achieve effective symptom control, all the above problems must be dealt with.

PALLIATIVE CARE, AS ALREADY defined in this paper, can in theory be used in any setting. However, in reality, the ethos of an institution will determine how effectively the principles are accepted and acted upon.

People mainly die in one of three settings: at home, in hospices (mainly cancer patients) or in general hospitals. Although research will say that more people die in hospital than at home, it is important to remember that most of the dying process takes place at home. Hospital admissions very often occur in the last few days of life, frequently because sufficient anticipation of difficulties was not shown by the professionals concerned.

To achieve a dignified death in one's own home is very often the wish of the dying and those close to them. It is possible to achieve but requires coordination and cooperation at the highest level from all the professionals. The risk of inter-professional feuding is always a possibility.

The practical needs of the informal carers are a major issue in this situation. The absolute exhaustion that can arise when one is caring, on a full-time basis, for a dying person who is emotionally close cannot be overestimated. The needs of these carers should be the primary concern of the professionals involved with the family. Good management and teamwork will allow people to die at home in a dignified manner, and undoubtedly it is the setting within which the patient and family can be most in control.

PALLIATIVE CARE EVOLVED OUT of hospices – and their ethos is one of providing terminal care in a caring and holistic manner which takes account of the patient's physical, psychological, spiritual and social needs.

However excellent this sort of care is in hospices, the fact is that most hospices care only for cancer sufferers, while more people die from other conditions such as circulatory disorders.

Another issue of concern for those who applaud the

139

palliative care offered in hospices is the growing tendency to offer conventional investigative treatments in hospices, thus in some way narrowing the gap between hospital and hospice.

Hospitals, because of their hierarchical structure and sheer physical orientation, are often the antithesis of palliative care centres and, indeed, the skills required to deal with dying rest uneasily with the curative ethos of medicine in these institutions.

It is possible, particularly in paediatric settings where the patient and family will be seen as an entity, to provide care tailored to the needs of the individual. However, the requirements of the acutely ill and the dying are so disparate as to be often irreconcilable. Unfortunately, in these circumstances, it is usually the dying and their family who suffer from things such as lack of privacy or acknowledgement of their emotional needs.

Pain-relief is an integral part of palliative care. Equally important is the creation of a support system providing social, emotional and spiritual support, which is built on a foundation of trust and openness and tailored to individual needs. The bedrock of the system is a support system for those providing care – whether professional or informal carers.

This approach differs fundamentally from the previous approach to the dying where control of information was the exclusive domain of the doctor. This paternalistic approach is summarised in the phrase 'doctor knew best'.

IF ONE IS TOTALLY COMMITTED to assessing each patient individually and tailoring care to fit their needs, palliative care as discussed in this paper is not inappropriate or inadvisable in any case. The concept of a 'good death' must be evaluated in relation both to the dying and the bereaved. Man is a social being and the dying of one affects others. If the experience of either is more distressful and traumatic than it needs to be then a 'good death' has not occurred. To the dying it is essential that a 'whole person' approach is used and a hospice-type philosophy is an ideal model for healthcare professionals who wish to use this approach.

This approach focuses firstly on symptom relief – can a person die in dignity if symptoms such as pain, nausea and breathlessness are not addressed?

Then the emotional needs of the dying must be addressed. People do not change because they are dying. Indeed, established personality traits tend to become more exaggerated and need to be acknowledged. Few die without experiencing anxiety and fear at some level, and they need to know that others are prepared to share this journey with them.

The pendulum is swinging to total honesty with the dying. An assessment must be made which includes a careful evaluation of what the dying person is communicating in both verbal and non-verbal ways. Some deal with their dying by avoiding the subject, some by other means. The choice is theirs to make. It is important to be alert to their needs and open to their choice.

COPING WITH DEATH

DR BRENDAN DOODY

DEATH OCCURS AT A particular time and at a particular place. It may have been anticipated, preceded by a long illness, or unexpected and sudden as the result of an accident. Grief is the reaction to the loss of the person. Mourning is the process that occurs after such a loss. The intensity of emotions, the nature of progress and the time to resolution differ from one individual to another. What I am endeavouring to do in this chapter is to describe the manifestations of 'normal grief', the phases of the mourning process, how this process can go wrong and in the event of this happening, where to turn to for help.

Following death, the survivors often experience a period of numbness, which helps them to disregard the fact that the loss has occurred for a period of time. It is almost as if the enormity of what has happened has not yet sunk in. The dazed condition was described by one widow as like being 'on automatic pilot'. At the same time, a number of practical arrangements need to be made and relatives contacted. The bereaved person needs time to take in what has happened and needs help with even the most simple of decisions. During this period, outbursts of extreme distress may break through, or the person may feel very ill.

Actually seeing the body may bring home what really has happened and it is important, where possible, for the family members to have an opportunity to do so. The funeral service may also have this effect, but has other important functions. It has the effect of drawing relatives, friends and neighbours close to the bereaved family, providing them with an important source of support. It gives the bereaved the opportunity to express their thoughts and feelings of grief.

The funeral can help the bereaved make sense of what has happened. This can be particularly true in the case of a sudden death when there has been no opportunity to anticipate or prepare for the event. For those with religious beliefs, it helps to place their bereavement in a meaningful perspective. And it has been shown that they cope better than those with no faith. However, it is also true that strong believers, whose view of God was that of a loving, protective father, found it hard to maintain this perspective following an untimely bereavement and were not helped by the possibility of reunion at some time in the future.

For some, the period of numbness and shock may continue for up to two weeks, by which time the funeral will have already taken place. It is also a time when the earlier level of support may be no longer available. Relatives and friends may have gained the impression that the bereaved person 'coped well' at the time of the funeral and is best left alone and not 'upset'. In fact, this could be the opposite of the person's actual needs.

THE SECOND PHASE OF mourning is characterised by a 'yearning' or 'pining' for the deceased and is accompanied by well-recognised patterns of feelings, ways of thinking and behaviours. However, not all of these symptoms will be experienced by any one person. The most common feeling found in bereavement is sadness, more often than not manifested by crying. However, other feelings can be less anticipated, confusing and distressing.

Death takes away the security we feel about the world. It can suddenly become an uncertain, almost dangerous place – no longer can anything be taken for granted. Loneliness is a frequent complaint, and the anxiety about one's ability to cope alone is accompanied by the realisation of your own mortality and the mortality of other people.

Anger is frequently experienced by survivors and can be one of the most confusing and distressing feelings. This anger is born out of frustration at not being able to prevent the death occurring. It can be directed at the deceased: one widow asked her dead husband 'Why did you leave me?' It can also be directed at the medical and nursing professionals. 'If only they looked after him properly' is often remarked. When such ill-directed expressions of anger are directed at family and friends in the early stages of grief, it can lead to quarrels and lasting antipathy between family members or friends. This, in turn, leads to a loss of support when it is most needed.

Guilt and self-reproach are commonly experienced – guilt about how they treated the person in the past (particularly if death occurred at a time when the relationship with the deceased was strained), or not taking the person to see the doctor sooner, for example. It is often the case that guilt centres around something that was neglected around the time of the death. More often than not, this guilt is irrational and will gradually be seen as such. This can be facilitated further by the support of other people.

When death occurs following a particularly long and painful illness, it is accompanied by a sense of relief that the suffering is over. However, surviving relatives may be left with a sense of guilt at having wanted the illness to end.

Thinking is preoccupied with thoughts of the deceased and may include obsessional thoughts of how to recover the lost person. There is a tendency to forget the negative aspects of the dead and a distorted idealised picture can be built up, which is often encouraged by society. This can, in turn, lead to increased feelings of guilt, as the bereaved blame themselves for any difficulties they had in the relationship with the deceased. This phase may also be marked by a sense of confusion and forgetfulness, such as laying a place at the table for the deceased many weeks after their death. Such experiences may cause the bereaved person to fear they are 'losing their mind'. This can be compounded by the experience of visual and auditory phenomena related to the deceased.

Transitory visual illusions may also occur, such as 'seeing' the bereaved approaching in the street, only to find when they get close that it is, in fact, somebody else. These illusions may include hearing the person opening the door, only to find that there is nobody there. Such experiences are not uncommon and usually occur in the early weeks following the bereavement.

Sleep disturbance may occur, manifesting itself as a difficulty getting to sleep or waking early in the morning. This gives rise to tiredness during the day and difficulty coping with life. Some people use alcohol as a sedative. However, its habit-forming potential can give rise to further problems. Studies have shown that the consumption of alcohol is increased following bereavement. Sleeping tablets prescribed by a doctor may be indicated and provide a safer alternative, but need to be used in a judicious manner as they also possess a habit-forming potential.

Dreams of the deceased may be pleasant in nature, in which the person is still alive. Dreams containing more disturbing imagery can occur, recreating the actual death and the helplessness of the dreamer to prevent events occurring.

A WAY OF REDUCING the pain of grief is to avoid all thoughts of the lost person and to avoid people and situations which could possibly act as reminders. Within the home, this can manifest itself with the removal of particularly evocative objects or photographs and not wanting to dispose of the person's clothing. Extreme social withdrawal reduces the chance of meeting a sympathetic person who might want to talk about the loss. Visiting the grave, which is a very pointed reminder, is avoided.

Another option is to move away for a period, or sometimes for good. Such behaviour may produce some short-term benefit. But to persist with such denial of the death will interfere with the grieving process and is ultimately unhelpful.

On the other hand, the bereaved may undertake forms of behaviour that remind them of the deceased, such as visiting places associated with the deceased or the actual place of death. Together with the carrying of mementos about with them, this can be seen as a fear on the part of the bereaved of losing memories of the deceased. With time, this will lessen in intensity.

Crying is often the most outward expression of grief and

is a way of relieving distress. We differ in our ability to express such emotion – to some it is a sign of weakness, others fear the reaction and possible criticism. Not surprisingly, it can be seen as reassuring by a bereaved person when those who are nearest show that they are not afraid to allow feelings of sorrow to emerge. Crying alone may be helpful, but not as effective as crying with someone who can provide support and help in identifying the meaning of the loss.

Bereavement also affects physical health. Studies of bereaved people have shown that their 'general health' has been worse following bereavement. The risk of serious illness is also increased, as is the risk of death. However, this is largely confined to the first six months of bereavement.

Not all the feelings and behaviours that have been outlined will be experienced by a bereaved person. Rather, they illustrate the diversity that can be experienced as part of normal grief.

DEATH NOT ONLY RESULTS in the loss of a loved one but also the roles that the person filled. It may take a number of months for the bereaved to realise what these roles actually were. For example, the loss of a husband forces new roles on the survivor – coming to terms with living alone, bringing up children alone and managing the family finances alone. Loss of a breadwinner frequently leads to financial hardship. The need to learn these new roles without the support of someone they had come to rely on, at a time when other family members are also bereaved and needing support, can place a major extra burden on the widow.

Gradually, a more realistic memory of the deceased develops, incorporating the bad points in addition to all the good ones. The sadness begins to lift and a process of disengagement occurs. This is not about giving up the relationship with the person who is lost. Rather, it is a process whereby the bereaved find an appropriate place for the deceased in their mind that allows them to move forward and function effectively in the world. This was described by Sigmund Freud in a letter to his friend Biswanger, whose son had died:

We find a place for what we lose. Although we know that after such a loss the acute stage of mourning will subside, we also know that we shall remain inconsolable and will never find a substitute. No matter what may fill the gap even if it be filled completely, it nevertheless remains something else.[1]

When does mourning finish? This is a difficult question to answer. It can be said to occur when the bereaved can truly accept that the person is gone and thoughts of the person do not produce pain. Of course, memories will always produce sadness, but the quality will not be as intense. How long this will take depends on a number of factors. The circumstances of the death, relationship with the deceased, availability of support, personality and previous life experience of an individual are all likely to be important determinants of the reaction to bereavement. Grief takes time. It does not follow a steady progress, but is punctuated by bad days. However, it cannot be avoided and the phrase 'time heals' does have some validity. Following the loss of someone with whom you had a close relationship, complete resolution may take at least a year and, for some, up to two years.

Some people fail to grieve, while others are not able to resolve their grief. Certain types of relationships with the deceased can cause difficulties, most frequently a relationship which was ambivalent and characterised by unexpressed hostility. On the other hand, relationships that were highly dependant can also pose problems.

Sudden and untimely deaths can, by the overwhelming sense of loss they produce at the time, cause the bereaved to delay their grief. This can last for years and may be triggered eventually by some other type of loss. This can also occur when one bereavement follows closely on another. The pain of further grief would be just too much to bear. When the loss is uncertain, for example when the body of the deceased is not recovered following a drowning, it can interfere with the initiation of grief.

1. Freud E.L., *Letters of Sigmund Freud*, Basic, New York, 1961.

Other factors which may complicate grief reactions include early parental loss and personality factors which affect one's ability to cope with stress or ability to form relationships.

Chronic grief reactions are said to occur when the grief is excessive in its duration and not coming to a conclusion. Frequently, such individuals are socially isolated and have great difficulty functioning without their loved one or finding anything in life to look forward to.

With time, as the reality of the loss becomes real, a person may begin to despair. A certain amount of pain is inevitable, but for a small number of bereaved this can become totally disabling and associated with feelings of worthlessness and thoughts of suicide. It is common to hear remarks such as 'I wouldn't care if I was dead', and they need not be taken too seriously. However, if a person has seriously thought of ending their own life, it needs to be taken seriously and help sought from the family doctor. If concern exists, it is better to ask, as asking about suicide does not increase the risk of it occurring. Such people usually, but not always, have a history of depression or other mental health disorders. When a depressive illness complicates bereavement, treatment with antidepressant medication may be indicated.

SOCIAL FACTORS PLAY AN extremely important part in the facilitation of the normal grieving process. At the time of the death, relatives, friends and neighbours call to the bereaved. Aside from the conventional expression of sympathy, communication can be difficult. This is not a situation in which there is a 'right thing' to say. It is best to say what one feels. Pity is not always well received. During the early phase of numbness and shock, the bereaved need practical help so they can have time to get their thoughts together. The funeral service draws the community together in support of the bereaved and can be extremely helpful in facilitating grief.

It is often after the funeral that the pangs of grief become most intense. It is now that the person needs a supportive listener who can accept the tendency of the bereaved to pour out feelings of anguish and anger. It may be necessary to indicate that such feelings are to be expected and not bottled up inside. In Shakespeare's play *Macbeth*, Malcolm says to Macduff:

Give sorrow words: the grief that does not speak whispers the o'erwrought heart, and bids it break.

Macbeth (1606) Act 4 Sc. 3.

However, too much probing can be unhelpful, as can conniving with the bereaved to avoid grief. What is necessary to accept is that a difficult and painful task has to be performed by the bereaved and that it cannot be rushed. Practical help is also needed to prepare the bereaved for their new roles and responsibilities.

During the period of mourning, society expects the bereaved to behave in a certain way. The bereaved person may also come to feel ostracised. It is quite common for neighbours and friends to avoid meeting or speaking with the bereaved. This arises out of fear about what they should say, fear of 'upsetting' the bereaved person and how they should react if this were to occur. Such experiences may lead the person to hide their grief as they come to believe that it is socially unacceptable. This is something that should not be allowed to happen.

It was once a custom in this country to wear a dark armband or dark-coloured dress which provided an outward sign of mourning for a prescribed period. Although this custom has fallen out of favour, it did have the advantage of sanctioning a period of mourning which helped the bereaved to feel more secure in their grief. Nowadays, without such a guide, unreasonable expectations can be placed on the bereaved as to when they should be 'getting over it'.

Outside of family and friends, members of the care-giving professions such as the clergy, doctors, public health nurses and social workers whose work brings them into contact with the bereaved, all have a role to play in counselling. They are particularly needed when a person is socially isolated, lacking in family and friends.

The family doctor has often been involved in the care of the person who has died, and this places the doctor in a good position to give help to the bereaved after the death has occurred. Questions about the illness and care given can be answered, the need to mourn the loss encouraged and reassurance provided as to what is normal. It can sometimes happen that physical symptoms similar to those suffered by the deceased are experienced by the bereaved. This does not imply that he or she is going to die of the same illness. Not surprisingly, the family doctor is consulted more frequently following a bereavement because of the increased likelihood of ill-health. Not every patient feels comfortable expressing the emotional difficulties that they are encountering, fearing that they are too 'trivial' to waste the busy doctor's time with. However, the family doctor can provide that sympathetic ear and help with problems that may arise during the grief reaction.

A visit by a member of the clergy is nearly always appreciated following a bereavement. He needs to show acceptance of the grief and the anger against God that may be expressed. The person's view of God may have been shattered and the promise of an ultimate reunion may be of little comfort. What is necessary is to become aware of the needs of the bereaved and remember that nobody can provide what is most desired – the return of the deceased. It is important that the initial visit is followed up by visits at intervals during the first year.

Other professionals who come into contact with the bereaved have the opportunity to play a similar role and should not undervalue the positive contribution that they can make. However, you do not need to be trained to be of help. What you have to do is show that you want to listen, to sit down and have that cup of tea.

Bereavement counselling can be of great benefit for those who need extra help. It may be provided by a professional, such as a doctor, a trained volunteer or by another bereaved person. This can take place on a 'one to one' basis or in a group setting. The goals of such therapy are to increase the reality of the loss, to help deal with emotions and experiences, to overcome particular difficulties that may arise, and to allow separation to take place. Groups can be particularly effective at providing support through shared experience. However, such groups may become a permanent refuge for some, rather than a means of achieving an objective.

Such services are becoming increasingly available throughout the country. By contacting the local citizens' information centre you can find out what is available in your area.

Grief is the pain of not having the person who is gone. Through this grief and the emotions of sadness, anger, fear, guilt and loneliness, we gradually learn to live without that person. We accept that the person is dead and not coming back. What is past is past and cannot be changed. It is possible to look forward again. This process takes time and needs the help and support of others. Acceptance is a positive and healthy step forward. It is accompanied by a sense of inner peace. This was described by St John Chrysostorn, a bishop living in the fourth century:

> *He whom we love and lose is no longer where he was before. He is now wherever we are.*

LIVING WITH DYING

DR TONY O'BRIEN

THE FOCUS OF MODERN healthcare is primarily directed towards prevention, early detection and cure of disease. The main objective of a national healthcare programme is not simply concerned with the eradication of disease, but rather strives to ensure that each individual is enabled to live a full and rewarding life in terms of his/her physical, emotional and social well-being. This is entirely proper and appropriate and is what most people expect from their health service.

Over the past century, we have witnessed dramatic improvements in our understanding of disease. The development of new drugs and technologies has opened up a vast new range of treatment options. Diseases which in the past were inevitably fatal, are now considered curable. Many of the infectious diseases which devastated communities a generation ago, are now well under control.

Whilst acknowledging and welcoming these many positive developments in medical science, we must also recognise the fact that, in many instances, patients cannot be cured of their disease. Despite all of the treatment options available, the disease will run a progressive course and will ultimately cause the death of the patient. Healthcare professionals and indeed society as a whole must consider their response to such patients and their families. Are they to be considered as failures, for whom nothing more can be done? On the contrary, they too must be assured of our continued commitment to their care, so that they also may live full and rewarding lives in terms of their physical, emotional and social well-being. These patients must not be abandoned or caused to feel that they have been abandoned.

Kearney put this issue into perspective when he wrote:

Patients with incurable illness must no longer be viewed as medical failures for whom nothing more can be done. They need palliative care, which does not mean a hand-holding second-rate soft option, but treatment, which most people will need at some point in their lives, and many from the time of diagnosis, demanding as much skill and commitment as is normally brought into preventing, investigating and curing illness.[1]

Indeed, it is precisely because the disease state cannot be cured or reversed that these patients must be assured of our continuing care and support. Wall expressed very similar sentiments when he wrote:

The immediate origins of misery and suffering need immediate attention while the long term search for basic cure proceeds.[2]

IN RECOGNITION OF THIS fact, and in response to the identified and perceived needs of patients and their families, the modern hospice movement has developed. Inspired by the pioneering work of Dame Cicely Saunders, at St Christopher's Hospice in London, the principles of hospice care have become firmly established in healthcare programmes throughout the world. Hospice care, or palliative care as it is now called, is concerned with the active treatment of patients and their families at a stage in their illness when the disease process is advanced and progressive, and when measures aimed at achieving a cure are shown to be inadequate.

Palliative care responds to the physical, psychological, social and spiritual needs of patients. It seeks to ensure that patients are provided with prompt and effective relief from pain and other distressing symptoms, and tries to create an environment in which patients are encouraged and enabled to live full, active and creative lives. In summary, the goal of palliative care is to achieve the highest possible quality of life

1. Kearney M., 'Palliative Care in Ireland', *Journal of the Irish College of Physicians and Surgeons*, 1991, 20 (3), p. 170.
2. Wall P. D., Editorial – 'Twenty-five Volumes of Pain', *Pain*, 1986; 25:1–4.

for both patient and family.

Palliative care is essentially a concept of care which has application in all care settings. Some patients will choose to be at home with their family, and will be comforted by their familiar surroundings. Others may prefer the reassurance that is offered by nurses and doctors in a hospital or hospice setting. The place of care is perhaps less important than the quality of care that is available. As the disease advances, it may well be necessary for a patient to receive care in a number of different settings, depending on the particular circumstances at that time. The health services must be sufficiently flexible and adaptive to ensure that patients can move easily and without delay from one care setting to another.

Family members should resist the temptation to make promises to keep their loved one at home in all circumstances. This promise, offered in good faith in the earlier stages of the illness, may become increasingly difficult to fulfil as the patient becomes weaker and requires more care. Ultimately, the patient's care and comfort may be compromised if family members feel committed to a promise that was made many months earlier, when the care needs were entirely different. Many patients will have the majority of their care undertaken at home and will die at home. For others, their needs may simply outstrip that which can be offered at home. The best setting for any patient, whether home, hospital or hospice, is the one which is best suited to their needs at any particular point in time. Admission to an in-patient unit must not be portrayed as a lack of care or concern on behalf of the family.

A DIAGNOSIS OF FAR-ADVANCED and progressive disease is a devastating and bewildering experience for most patients and families. It has the capacity to create enormous stresses for even the most stable and loving of families, and the shock waves will reverberate throughout the entire family structure. The stability and sense of balance within the family group is severely tested.

It is impossible to consider the impact of this news on patients unless we consider them in the context of their family. Patients do not exist in isolation. If anyone of us is found to have a serious illness, the impact of that illness will affect, directly or indirectly, a whole range of people, including immediate family, relatives and friends.

When using the term 'family' in this regard, I do not simply confine my comments to blood relatives. Not infrequently, the 'family carer' who is closest and most important to the patient, is not a blood relative. Changes in our society and family structures require us to redefine our concept of family. The term 'family' is therefore used in its broadest context and essentially includes anybody who is significant in the life of the patient. As people in our society have become increasingly mobile, it is not unusual for family members to live quite a distance from the person who is ill. This creates its own problems in terms of offering support, whilst at the same time trying to fulfil work and family commitments at home.

The recognition that a family member is going to die creates a crisis as family members try to find new ways of coping. The news frequently evokes a complex array of powerful and sometimes conflicting emotions. The panic and fear associated with the new circumstances may cause people to retreat into very polarised positions, and some may seek to deny their new reality. The prospect of letting go, of finding new ways of functioning and relating to one another, of filling the gap and the role previously fulfilled by the ill person, may prove too difficult to achieve. Serious differences of opinion may surface, resulting in a lack of accommodation of other views, and ultimately progressing to suspicion and mistrust.

FOR PATIENTS TOO, THIS is a time of rapid readjustment. In addition to the stresses of coping with the effects of the illness and its associated treatments, they will also feel some very powerful emotions. Feelings of loss predominate – the loss of role and status, loss of a future life, loss of family, loss of independence, etc. For many, one of the most difficult aspects to accept is the enforced dependency on others.

Many relatives, when faced with this situation, may seek

to protect the patient by limiting the amount of information that is made available to them. On occasion, the relatives may insist that the patient is given frankly misleading information regarding diagnosis and ultimate prognosis. This desire to protect is entirely understandable but can have far-reaching and very negative implications for the patient and for the family's ability to cope.

This desire to protect by censoring information will inevitably result in a breakdown of communication. Patients will know when those closest to them are being less than honest. A vast amount of precious time and energy is devoted to maintaining the pretence. This is both unhelpful and unnecessary, as it so often happens that the patient is already fully aware of their situation. The net result of this conspiracy of silence is to introduce a barrier to communication which will cause the patient to feel increasingly isolated from those nearest to them.

In such circumstances, it is virtually impossible for the patient to voice their fears and concerns and to receive appropriate reassurance. An impenetrable barrier is erected between the patient and those closest to them. Confronted by an ever more elaborate web of deceit and deception, the patient is plunged into a state of loneliness and isolation.

IN TIMES OF DISTRESS, it is vitally important that families try to increase their links with each other in a very definite 'bridge-building' exercise. The need to support and to be supported is paramount. Failure to build bridges will result in the creation of a vulnerable and maladaptive family. The family group, in a well-intentioned but perhaps misguided attempt to protect one another, and perhaps inspired by a misplaced sense of loyalty, create an environment in which it is not acceptable to show feelings or to voice concerns. Consequently, individual family members may feel extremely confused, and this confusion may be compounded by feelings of guilt, anger, resentment, frustration and sadness.

Caring for a patient with advanced disease will often require a redistribution of roles. The ill person may previously have functioned as breadwinner or homemaker and may experience considerable pain associated with the loss of this role. Others may need to assume responsibility for some aspects of the ill person's role, although care should be taken to ensure that we do not take away these roles prematurely. Families will need to demonstrate considerable creativity and enterprise to ensure that the patient is enabled to contribute to family life in some useful way, for as long as possible.

This redistribution of roles is not without problems. For example, a husband who previously did not contribute much to household duties, may find himself trying to cope with cooking, shopping, helping with homework, in addition to sustaining a full-time job. Similarly, coping with the family finances, insurances, etc., may pose a most intimidating challenge to the uninitiated. The situation is further complicated by the fact that the patient may set very high standards and not infrequently will voice their criticism when the carer's best efforts fail to reach the desired standard. A negotiated solution is best and the patient will need to accept compromise.

When families fail to make bridges and establish a system of dealing with their new situation, a number of problems will arise. Not infrequently, a conspiracy of fear and denial becomes established, which results in people holding on to difficult, indeed agonising burdens. This sense of isolation and unfamiliarity causes people to distance themselves from one another. The potential for misunderstanding and suspicion is obvious.

Family members may feel that they alone are carrying an unfair burden of responsibility and are not receiving an adequate level of input and support from others. These pent up feelings will result in angry explosions within the family, causing much hurt and distress. Rather than uniting in a common cause, families become increasingly fragmented and disparate. The result is the creation of a whole maladaptive family, or perhaps a previously established pattern of maladaptive behaviour is simply reinforced.

Ideally, families will take steps to ensure that this situation does not occur, or if it is already established, then some corrective action is necessary. This will involve an openness and a willingness to share both strengths and vulnerabilities, which is not at all easy. Families might usefully sit down together to examine what is happening and to confront the impact that this is having on each of their lives. Remember that the loss of any person will be a very different experience for all involved, as they will each have a different and unique relationship with that person, and each will be at a different stage in their own lives. For example, when a man in his forties dies, his wife will lose a husband, his children will lose a father, his parents will lose a son, his siblings will lose a brother and his friends will lose a friend and confidante.

The very fact that families are willing to sit down together is a statement of their concern for each other and demonstrates a willingness to offer support and to be supported. A family meeting such as this generates openness and creates the possibility of truth being shared. Of course, it takes courage to engage in such discussions, particularly if people feel that there are issues which they would prefer not to recognise or address. However, even one such meeting can help to generate confidence in a situation that feels totally out of control, and where a maladaptive pattern of behaviour is already established.

It is important to recognise that sitting down to examine what is happening within a family does not, in itself, create difficult issues. The issues are already there. Conversely, by placing our heads in the sand, the issues do not disappear. If anything, they are apt to take on even more monstrous and frightening proportions.

WHEN DISCUSSING THE NEEDS of families, it is important to recognise and address the specific needs of children. Children will harvest information from a variety of sources, much of it from unspoken communications. Based on their own limited experience of life and working within their own contextual framework, the child will try to understand what is happening within their family structure. Not surprisingly, their conclusions are frequently flawed and commonly their fantasies are considerably worse than the reality.

Family members may wish to protect children from the pain of loss but in so doing may further isolate them and add to their distress. Children who are facing the death of a parent have the capacity to arouse strong emotions in all of us. Somehow, their innocence and their vulnerability make us conscious of the risk of causing injury or further harm. However, in a well-intentioned but misguided attempt to protect children, we may leave them totally isolated and unprotected from their fears and their fantasies.

It is important to explore the child's thoughts about their experiences as fully as possible and respond to their individual needs. It is not uncommon for young children to feel that, in some way, they are responsible for their parent's illness. They must be properly reassured in this regard. Children will need the opportunity to ask questions, to receive information and reassurance, and to express and share their feelings in a safe and supportive environment.

Barbara Monroe reminds us that information should be given gradually to children, perhaps over many days or weeks. 'Mummy is ill. Mummy is very ill. Mummy is so ill the doctors are not sure they can make her better. Mummy is so ill that the doctors can't make her better. Mummy is so ill that she is going to die'.[3] When talking to children, we should use simple words which the child can understand. Avoid terms such as 'Daddy has gone to sleep' or 'Angels came in the night and took Daddy away'. This figurative language can create confusion in the mind of a child. Simple, factually correct language is best. As in the case of adults, we must resist the temptation to lie to children and must not make promises that we cannot keep.

In addition to information exchange, children will also need reassurance, particularly about their own continuing care. They need the opportunity to express their feelings and to have these acknowledged. On occasions, when a parent dies, the surviving parent is often grieving so much themselves that they are unable to understand the need to grieve

3. Monroe B., 'Supporting children facing bereavement', in *Hospice and Palliative Care – an Inter-disciplinary Approach*, Edward Arnold, London, 1990, p. 80.

in their child. Children need space for their feelings and questions. They also feel pain. It is always worth ensuring that the child's teacher is aware of illness in the home and regular contact should be maintained between the family and the teachers.

IN THE COURSE OF any far-advanced and progressive disease, a point will be reached when it becomes clear that time is short and death is imminent. Many adults in contemporary society have never witnessed a death. They will need the opportunity to ask questions and to be prepared for what is about to happen. They must have information on the normal processes of dying, if only to ensure that they will recognise what is happening as 'normal'. Information serves to empower, and families will cope with a dying relative much more confidently if they have been adequately prepared.

Whether death occurs in the home or in an institutional setting, the care of a dying person should be undertaken in a simple, calm and unhurried fashion. Family members should have the opportunity to become involved in the care of the patient to whatever extent that they feel comfortable. Creating the opportunity for family members to become involved does not equate with implying that they should be involved. Yet many will derive considerable comfort from participating in the practical nursing care of their loved one, by helping with washing, moistening lips, etc.

For some family members, it is vitally important that they are present at the moment of death. Equally, others will feel that they have already contributed as much as they possibly can to their loved one and would prefer not to be present at the moment of death. There are no 'rights' or 'wrongs' in this situation and this is clearly a matter of personal choice. In order to be in a position to make an informed choice, people will require and appreciate information about what to expect, how symptoms will be controlled, the changes that will occur in the final hours and minutes of life and what will happen immediately after the death.

Even at this late stage, there may be important things which family members may need to say to their loved one.

Some may simply need to say 'I love you' and 'Thank you for all of the times that we have shared'. Others may simply want to be physically with the person who is dying for as long as possible. Within families, it is important to recognise that individuals may need some period of quiet time alone with the patient so that they have an opportunity to say their goodbyes and other important things in private.

Just as for birth, there is tremendous uncertainty around the exact timing of death. Doctors and nurses can predict the timing of a death with some limited degree of accuracy, but very often it happens that a patient will die sooner than anticipated or indeed may live for many hours or perhaps some days after death was expected. It is, therefore, impossible for family members to ensure that they will be with their loved one at the time of death. Even in instances where family members have maintained a twenty-four hour vigil at the bedside for many days, it sometimes happens that death occurs during those few minutes when a relative slips out for a cup of coffee or a cigarette.

REGARDLESS OF HOW MUCH one has been prepared, the moment of death is often a time of profound emotional and, sometimes, physical shock. At this time, family members will need the opportunity and the privacy to absorb what has happened, to say their own goodbyes and to express their emotions in their own way. This is an opportunity for the family to unite in giving and receiving comfort and support. Families can take their time at this stage and must not feel pressurised to start making numerous phone calls and detailed arrangements. A close family friend will be able to offer some practical help in making phone calls, arrangements, etc.

Almost invariably, families unite in some form of prayer at this time. Uniting in a common purpose and comforted by the familiarity of the words of the prayers, families are able to contain the shock and panic brought on by the death. Prayer is important for most families and can provide considerable comfort. After a period, family members may wish to help with washing and dressing the body, and if so, should be encouraged and enabled to do so. It is important, particularly in the institutional setting, to ensure that families are not made to feel excluded by the professionalism of staff members.

In the days following a death, family members are often preoccupied with dealing with the funeral arrangements and meeting with many relatives and friends. The family may well need to make some space for their own needs at this time. The death of their loved one marks the ending of a very important phase in their life, yet also marks the beginning of a new phase.

Families need to recognise that the process of bereavement is characterised by a bewildering array of physical and emotional experiences. They are likely to experience strong and conflicting feelings of love and resentment, sadness and anger. Commonly, their thoughts are preoccupied with hundreds of 'if onlys'. If only he had seen the doctor sooner, if only they had operated, if only they hadn't operated, if only they gave him more chemotherapy, if only he had not had chemotherapy, etc. They need to understand that intense feelings of sadness and pain are common and that they are not alone in these feelings. Grief is a normal and inevitable human journey, not an illness. Most people will successfully accomplish the tasks of grief with the help of their family, friends and local community. As a society, we must recognise that the process of grieving takes considerably longer than we sometimes appreciate. The disappearance of a formally recognised period of mourning does not take away the need of the individual to grieve.

Anything which is scarce becomes precious. In palliative care the commodity in scarce supply is time. During the final stages of life, time becomes extremely precious. There is enormous potential at this time for people to examine the most fundamental aspects of their lives. There is an opportunity for people to explore their relationships with themselves, with their families and friends and with their God. It is a time of coming together, of uniting, of giving and receiving, of supporting and of being supported; it is a time of healing, a time to say important things, to hear important

162

things. It is a family time, and individuals and families can choose how they want to use this time. This facet is worthy of deep consideration, as mistakes cannot be rectified later.

FURTHER INFORMATION

The following are some useful contact numbers and addresses which provide free advice, referral or support.

Many of the organisations have branches in towns and cities throughout the country. Others, such as Bethany groups, are confined solely to the Dublin region.

The public services in Ireland do not provide bereavement counselling. However, hospital chaplains and hospital social workers may be of help in individual cases.

For information on local support groups it may be useful to check with your community centre, health centre, citizens' information centre, or check the notice-boards at your parish church, your local library or at your doctor's office.

Parish-based bereavement support groups are located in many parts of the country. They provide an understanding and compassionate environment for those who have suffered bereavement.

THE EDITOR

BEREAVEMENT

Bereavement Counselling Service, c/o St Ann's Church, Dawson Street, Dublin 2. Phone: (01) 6767727.
Bethany Bereavement Support Group, Sheelagh's Well, Bellevue, Delgany, Co. Wicklow. Phone: (01) 2872507.
The Bereavement Society – Coping with Grief, 5 Cuil Fearne, Mullinarry, Carrickmacross, County Monaghan. Phone: (042) 64000.
Compassionate Friends for Bereaved Parents, 18 Kilbarrack Avenue, Raheny, Dublin 5. Phone: (01) 8324618.

CHILDREN

Irish Stillbirth and Neonatal Death Society (ISANDS), Carmichael House, 4 North Brunswick Street, Dublin 7. Phone: (01) 2831910, 8203130.
Irish Sudden Infant Death Association, Carmichael House, 4 North Brunswick Street, Dublin 7. Freefone Support Helpline: 1-800-391391, General Office: (01) 8732711.
Miscarriage Association of Ireland, 27 Kenilworth Road, Dublin 6. Phone: (01) 4972938 (5-6 pm).
Association for the Welfare of Children in Hospital, c/o Brookwood, Tubber, Lucan, Co. Dublin. Phone: (01) 2889278.

WIDOWS' ASSOCIATIONS

National Association of Widows in Ireland, 12 Upper Ormond Quay, Dublin 7. Phone: (01) 6770977, 6770513.
Widows' Association, Boylan Community Centre, Dún Laoghaire, Co. Dublin. Phone: (01) 2809972.

LONG-TERM ILLNESS

The Alzheimer Society of Ireland, St John of God Hospital, Stillorgan, Co. Dublin. Phone: (01) 2881282.
Irish Cancer Society Helpline, 5 Northumberland Road, Dublin 4. Freefone: 1-800-200-700.
Irish Association for Spina Bifida and Hydrocephalus, Old Nangor Road, Clondalkin, Dublin 22. Phone: (01) 4572326.
Helpful Hands, 124 Meadowvale, Blackrock, Co. Dublin. Phone: (01) 2892163.

SUICIDE

The Friends of the Suicide Bereaved, P.O. Box 162, Cork. Phone: (021) 294318.

MURDER

Victim Support, 29/30 Dame Street, Dublin 2. Phone: (01) 6798673.

GENERAL

Parentline: Organisation for Parents Under Stress, Carmichael House, North Brunswick Street, Dublin 7. Phone: (01) 8733500.

The Samaritans, 112 Marlborough Street, Dublin 1. Freefone: 1-850-60-90-90, or (01) 8727700.

The Mental Health Association of Ireland, Mensana House, 6 Adelaide Street, Dún Laoghaire, Co. Dublin. Phone: (01) 2841166.

FURTHER READING

MOST BOOKS ON THE subject of death are written from a British or American perspective. The content is seldom geared to the cultural, ethical or medical ethos that pertains in Ireland.

The following is a selection of some of the best publications available. These are drawn from many nationalities and are readily available in most Irish bookshops.

Two of the classic works on the topic are as follows:

Elisabeth Kübler-Ross, *On Death and Dying*, Routledge, London and New York, 1992.

Colin Murray Parkes, *Bereavement: Studies of Grief in Adult Life*, Penguin Books, London, 1991.

Other excellent books on grief and death are:

Judy Tatelbaum, *The Courage to Grieve*, Cedar Books, London, 1993.

Carol Lee, *Good Grief*, Fourth Estate, London, 1994.

Dorothy Rowe, *The Courage to Live*, Fontana, London, 1991.

Nigel Llewellyn, *The Art of Dying*, Reaktion Books, London, 1991.

Philippe Aries, *The Hour of Our Death*, Allen Lane, London, 1977.

There is a substantial body of literature on the death of a child. In particular, there is one very helpful book which is Irish published:

Anna Farmar, *Children's Last Days*, Town House, Dublin, 1992.

Other publications on child death include:

Nancy Kohner and Alix Henley, *When a Baby Dies*, Pandora Press, London, 1991.

Barbara Ward and Associates, *Exploring Feelings, Loss and Death with Under 11's*, Good Grief Publishers, Middlesex, 1992.

The following are two highly recommended books on death and old age:
Elaine Murphy, *Death and Mental Illness in Old Age*, Papermac, London, 1986.
Alan Jacques, *Understanding Dementia*, Churchill Livingstone, Edinburgh, 1988.

A most interesting work on reaction to parental death was recently published in the United Kingdom. Contributors to the book include Maeve Binchy, Bruce Kent and Shusha Guppy. They describe their personal experiences and reactions following the death of a parent. The book is titled:
Jane McLoughlin (Editor), *On the Death of a Parent*, Virago Press, London, 1994.

Finally, there is a most valuable booklet for parents whose babies died around the time of birth. The booklet is called *A Little Lifetime*. It is published by the Health Education Bureau and The Irish Stillbirth and Neonatal Death Society and is available from the society's headquarters (see Further Information). It is free to bereaved parents or relatives of bereaved parents.

COLM KEANE

Nervous Breakdown

Edited by
Colm Keane

Most Irish families have at one time or another been affected by the bewildering consequences of 'nervous breakdown'. The symptoms and manifestations include depression, panic attacks, addictions, phobias, obsessions, sexual problems and difficulties eating and sleeping. These may result from anxiety, stress, trauma, family pressures, or from events such as job loss or bereavement. If you or your family have experienced any of these problems then this book will be of interest to you.

Nervous Breakdown is a companion to the RTE Radio 1 series of the same name. The book is prepared in an 'easy to read' style and is aimed at the non-expert. It offers simple advice on how to cope with the pressures and stresses of everyday life and it gives practical advice on the treatments available.

Contributors include some of Ireland's most eminent psychologists, psychiatrists and therapists.

When Food Becomes Your Enemy
Anorexia, Bulimia and Compulsive Overeating

Gillian Moore-Groarke and Sylvia Thompson

Anorexia, bulimia and compulsive overeating have become serious problems, with many families having to cope with the trauma of a son or daughter suffering from an eating disorder.

When Food Becomes Your Enemy is the first Irish book to tackle this complex subject. The authors explain simply and clearly:

* how anorexia, bulimia or compulsive overeating can take over your life
* why an eating problem is really only a symptom of deeper unease within the person.

Case histories illustrate the painful process from the initial stages to recovery, with sufferers illuminating in an honest and forthright way what is really going on *when food becomes your enemy*.

Create Your Own Health Patterns

John Fitzpatrick CSSp

Disease has to be understood in its literal sense dis-ease – a lack of ease and an expression of conflict. In general we create our own sickness and if we are capable of creating our own sickness then we are capable of recreating our own health. Once inner peace and harmony are re-established nature has the power to repair itself and good health should ensue.

Fr John Fitzpatrick sees every human being as having the innate ability to heal both self and others. Healing takes place in all cultures, within all belief systems and among all types of people. In some this ability is developed to a greater degree. It is an ability which can be enhanced and developed through practice and through the use of certain disciplines.

The Spirit of Tony de Mello
A Handbook of Meditation Exercises

John Callanan, S.J.

This book captures the essence and spirit of Tony
de Mello. He was a great teacher. Some said he was
a dangerous one. He constantly challenged himself,
the world within which he lived and those he came
into contact with. For some this element of
challenge was both unsettling and confusing. Tony
said that our security does not lie in thoughts or
ideas, no matter how profound. Neither does it lie
in traditions – no matter how hallowed. Security
can only reside in an attitude of mind and a
readiness to reflect deeply, thus subjecting any and
every belief to rigorous questioning.

So Tony urged people to question, question,
question. Questions often make us uncomfortable.
They do, however, force us to reflect and thus
ensure our growth.

John Callanan has started the book with an
opening chapter on the basics of prayer. Then he
moves on to try and give a flavour of the ideas and
themes which gave so much zest and life to Tony
de Mello's presentation. The exercises in this book
are based on the prayer-style which Tony himself
developed during his retreats.

An Easy Guide to Meditation

Roy Eugene Davis

Meditation is the natural process to use to release tension, reduce stress, increase awareness, concentrate more effectively and be open to life. In this book you will learn how to meditate correctly for inner growth and spiritual awareness. Specific guidelines are provided to assist the beginner as well as the more advanced meditator. Here are proven techniques used by accomplished meditators for years: *prayer, mantra, sound–light contemplation, ways to expand consciousness and to experience transcendence.*

Benefits of correct meditation practice include: deep relaxation, stress reduction, inner calm, improved powers of intelligence, and strengthening of the immune system. People in all walks of life can find here the keys to living life as it was meant to be lived.

Body-Mind Meditation
A Gateway to Spirituality

Louis Hughes, OP

You can take this book as your guide for a fascinating journey that need not take you beyond your own hall door. For it is an inward journey, and it will take you no further than God who, for those who want him as a friend, lives within. On the way to God-awareness, you will be invited to experience deep relaxation of body and mind.

Body-Mind Meditation can help you become a more integrated balanced person. It is an especially helpful approach to meditation if the pace of life is too fast for you, or if you find yourself frequently tense or exhausted.

The Way of a Healer

Peter Gill

The Way of a Healer deals with different aspects of healing, and the way that spiritual healing works in the lives of people. Healing means health, and health is wholeness. That word wholeness implies a number of separate parts coming together to make a complete whole. We are accustomed to the concept of body, mind and soul, and unless these different aspects of ourselves function together in harmony we have disharmony or dis-ease. If that condition of dis-ease is allowed to continue un-qchecked, ultimately we have disease or illness. Spiritual healing works at the physical, mental, emotional and spiritual levels of a person.

Today we stand upon the brink of the darkest age that could yet befall mankind, or, with a change of consciousness, upon the edge of a new and wonderful dawn to herald in a golden age. What that age will be depends upon what we make of it now. The immediate need is for a concept which will integrate us with the life of the solar system and, through the solar consciousness, link us with the life of the universe and the word of God. Our thinking must become much more expansive to embrace, not only humankind as we know it, but also the angel, elemental and nature kingdoms, and other realms not normally perceived by our physical sense.

Born to Die?

Mary Butler

Mary Butler went into labour prematurely with her second child. The baby was born two days later with a rare congenital abnormality. It was two weeks before Mary knew for certain that it was a boy.

Born to Die? tells the story of this rare baby: the struggle to keep him alive; the surgery carried out by a dedicated medical team. It is also the story of Mary, her husband Rick and their families, and how they tried to cope with the emotional trauma of this period.